THAT FRIDAY IN EDEN

THAT FRIDAY IN EDEN

by Alberta Mazat

Pacific Press Publishing Association
Boise, Idaho
Oshawa, Ontario
Montemorelos, N.L., Mexico

Printed in the United States of America

Cover photo by Photofile
Designed by Ichiro Nakashima

Library of Congress Cataloging in Publication Data

Mazat, Alberta, 1919-

That Friday in Eden.

1. Sexual disorders. 2. Marriage. 3. Sex (Theology)

I. Title.

RC556.M39 613.9'6 80-25391

ISBN 0-8163-0401-7

84 85 86 87 88 89 • 6 5 4 3 2

To my husband,
who has shared and enhanced
my own sexuality for thirty-seven years.

Contents

Prologue I

The wise man spoke of what awed him:

"There be three things which are too wonderful for me,
Yea, four which I know not:
The way of an eagle in the air;
The way of a serpent upon a rock;
The way of a ship in the midst of the sea;
And the way of a man with a maid."

And, indeed, the way of an eagle in the air is splendid as it dives, swoops, and soars. A mortal can scarcely bear the longing to be able to exercise the freedom and the exuberance that such movement must provide.

The amazing serpent's ability to glide with ease and purpose over varied terrains, the meticulously patterned coat out of which it slips as enchantingly as a bride from a wedding gown—how mysterious! How inexplicable!

And properly confounding is the ship, plowing tirelessly and steadily through dark waters. Perhaps the wise man as a lad heard fascinating tales of that ship, that ark made after God's superb pattern, which carried a zoological melange and eight human landlubbers to safety during that cataclysmic event. No proper descendant of Noah could have felt anything but pride, excitement, and awe in recalling the guiding of that precious cargo into the cove made by the tops of the mountains, where it gently settled to the ground as the water receded.

What else could complete this set of wondrous observations? Does the wise man hesitate to ponder? Perhaps only to make the decision to add one more astonishment. He turns now to human relationships and chooses the way of a man with a maid.

It all began on a Friday in Eden with a young couple. The way of a maid and a man became an interaction of one-anotherness. It became a joyous congress of two lovers, completing one-fleshness as God intended.

I have addressed this book to this fourth wonder. I hope to provide a way of understanding the sexual aspects of the marital relationship which will encourage communication between wives and husbands. I respond here to requests to put into written form the materials I have presented in talks, workshops, and seminars.

My hearers have generally been Seventh-day Adventists. To them, then, this book is particularly directed. If it serves to enhance a feeling of joyousness in the pursuit of God's plan for sexuality, I will have been well rewarded for the time spent.

It Was on a Friday

The first four days had passed. From an earth "without form, and void" had sprung light, skies, seas, and a carpet of plants and grasses. Trees, shrubs, and vines accentuated and beautified, and to much of the flora the gift of flowering was entrusted. The scene brought to mind is one of consummate beauty. But even as I allow my imagination to enjoy this panorama, one thought persists: it is so quiet.

Rest one more "evening and morning" and then behold! The lands, seas, and air are alive with animal life of infinite variety. From the majestic to the miniature, from the colorful to the camouflaged, from the lithe to the leisurely—something to delight every sense.

Life abounds on a planet, spoken into existence by the Creator, who now puts Himself once more to work! "So God created man in his own image, in the image of God created he him; male and female created he them." Genesis 1:27.

This creation was "feeling." I like to think of the omniscient God bending over the rich earth He chose to use as the medium for man. Carefully He formed the head, including all the detail. The neck, the broad shoulders, the muscular arms, the amazingly engineered hand, which was to be capable of so many meticulous movements—all carefully sculptured. The symmetrical torso and then strong legs and feet, all minutely complete.

Now comes the moment! God breathed into Adam's nostrils "the breath of life; and man became a living soul." Genesis 2:7. An instant person! How did Adam wake up from a deep sleep and find out he is an adult, with no infancy, childhood, or adolescence to mold him into the prime of young manhood? What happens to his thinking when he discovers he just *is*? Did his mind find this as difficult to comprehend as mine does? (That's just one of the things I want to discuss with Adam someday!)

The first thing Adam looked upon was God, somehow perceiving in His gaze infinite love and joy. And somehow Adam perceives himself as a person and feels God's approval and anticipation. What did they say to each other? Did God explain to Adam the newness of this creative venture? Did He tell Adam how He had spoken into existence the things all about Him but had lovingly formed Adam with His own hands? Did He discuss the relationship that would exist between Him and Adam and what that relationsthip would mean to each of them, what the ultimate plan for this small part of the universe was?

Perhaps during the first conversation with his Maker, Adam noticed other living beings in this garden spot. Perhaps he spotted a shy fawn gazing at them from nearby bushes. Or maybe a teasing monkey or a noisy blue jay captured his attention. God might have explained to him how the precious quality known as "life" had been imparted to a gamut of land animals, large and small, as well as water-dependent and air-bound creatures. I like to think how Adam might have marveled at the softness of the alpaca's coat, the toughness of the elephant's back, the lean strength of a sinewy leopard, the engaging appeal of a koala bear's gaze. How God must have enjoyed explaining to him the portable "cradle" carried by a female kangaroo, the architectural talents of an oriole, and the cavorting of a dolphin. What great companionship God and Adam must have shared—just as God had envisioned.

At some time during these pristine hours Adam came to realize that though many other beings shared life with him, none was quite like himself. As they strolled through the garden, perhaps he kept looking beyond the next grove of trees, the next azalea clump for a form of life like himself. "But for Adam no suitable helper was found." Genesis 2:20 N.I.V. No one with the same intellectual powers or the same emotional makeup, no one with the same spiritual potential. And though in a perfect state, Adam felt a lack of completeness.

I like to think that when God saw Adam's realization of this need, He perceived the ideal time had come to complete His creation. God's realization that it was not good for man to be alone was not an afterthought, a decision prompted by an unforeseen need. This joining of male and female in a human relationship was always in His plan, and now was the time to bring it about. God could have created Adam and Eve simultaneously, but He did not. Perhaps He knew there would be times when Adam would need to remember how lonely it was without Eve and how much he needed her to complete his wholeness.

Now God put Adam to sleep—the first general anesthetic. With Adam awake he could have painlessly extracted that rib as a basis for Eve's creation. But beyond the contribution of a rib Adam was not to have any part in this creative act, not even one of passive observation. He could never boast, "I witnessed . . ." which could, conceivably, give a feeling of advantage over his wife. This was God's creative act and God's alone, and Adam slept through it. Again God goes through the procedure of building a body, this time with part of His first created being, thus establishing the beautiful sybolism of their oneness in reality. The head is formed, the arms and shoulders, breasts, and remaining body trunk, all in accurate detail, then the lower extremities. There are differences in these two creations which were not arbitrary. God's intent was that these two primal creatures were to complement, to fill, to complete one another—physically, emotionally, and spiritually.

Adam still sleeps as God carefully crafts to His satisfaction this woman. The Bible says succinctly, "And he brought her to the man." Verse 22. So much left to the imagination! Did He gently awaken Adam? Or did He talk to Eve first and acquaint her with herself? Was Adam aware that when he awakened he would be presented with a companion? We only know that "he brought her to the man." what a meeting! There stood Eve—beautiful, expectant. Beside her Adam—amazed, overjoyed. There stood God—gratified, delighted.

What was Adam's first verbal comment, I wonder. Someone has suggested, and I think not irreverently, that he sighed a rapturous "Wow!"—or whatever the Edenic-language equivalent might be! Somewhere during that conversation, we know that Adam made the profound statment, "This is now bone of my bones and flesh of my flesh; she shall be called 'woman,' for she was taken out of man." Verse 23. The Bible account further states, "The man and his wife were both naked, and they felt no shame." Shame, you see, was introduced by Satan, not God.

Then, since merely being together was not a significant enough phenomenon to begin a relationship as important as marriage, there was a ceremony to mark the beginning of their intimate relationship. How I wish we knew more about this! With a woman's curiosity, I am anxious to know about so many details. The music for instance, for celestial music always seemed to accompany important affairs, that is, creation, first advent, return to heaven of the redemmed. Did it consist of choirs, ensembles, or solos? I wonder what the homily consisted of in addition to this dictum: "For this reason a man will leave his father and mother and be united to his wife, and they will become one flesh." Perhaps it was necessary to explain about fathers and mothers. And maybe it was during the ceremony that God indeed explained to them what one-fleshness meant. Then God blessed them and said to them, "Be fruitful and increase in number; fill the earth and subdue it. Rule over the fish of the sea and the birds of the air and over every living creature that moves on the ground." Chapter 1:28. A good bit of explanation was necessary, however, to make that message meaningful to them. God would not give a brand-new human pair with no previous experience such a short command as "Be fruitful and multiply" and leave it without further explanation. God has always given His children all they need to know for an abundant life, and in the area of being fruitful and multiplying, they needed to know all there was to know.

How I wish I could know the words that God used to describe to them the beauty of sexual intimacy. What concepts did He employ as He explained all about His plan for their physical and emotional love experience—its nature, its permanence, its exclusivity, and its procreative ability? I am sure He used terms they could understand, not veiled references that left them wondering what He meant. As He explained in its lovely purity the plan for their bodies to unite in one flesh in the ultimate act of communication, how deeply thrilled they must have been.

Think of it, then, these two perfect human beings fresh from the hand of God, vibrant bodies with every nerve and nerve ending perfectly attuned, every exquisitely wrought muscle in perfect coordination, intellects free from all cultural and social hang-ups, spirits adoring their Creator and one another.

They had never had well-meaning parents act with embarrassment, horror, or stumbling when talking about sexual concepts. No one had ever told Eve that the genital parts of her body were dirty or shameful. No one had slapped Adam's hand when it first reached curiously and exploratively to his genitals. No one had intentionally or unintentionally frightened them about their sexual feelings or body processes. No one had given them spoken or unspoken messages about sex being dirty, funny, secret, suspect. No peers had supplied them with giggling, guessing misinformation. No, none of this. Just two perfect bodies, uncluttered minds, and selfless spirits loving one another. What a glorious wedding experience! And all according to God's plan.

Sometimes we get the impression that God made female and male parts but people found out what to do with them all by themselves—and that it must have surprised God to see how pleasurable it is! We have long neglected study of the aspects of physical love. Silence has somehow been seen as sanctity, and prudery as holiness. It is difficult for many people to perceive sexuality and holiness as being compatible.

But the Bible is very frank about sexual topics. So much so that these parts of the Bible were sometimes withheld from people in former times so they would not be led astray. A straightforward translation of the Bible was considered vulgar in Victorian times. In 1833 Webster issued an ammended King James Version which deleted such shocking words as *womb, fornication,* etc. In this version Noah no longer "spilled his seeds" which in itself is euphemistic, but "he frustrated the purpose."

This version no longer receives much attention today. But there still lingers among many of us a suspect feeling about the properness of our sexuality. I have had some people tell me that they cannot understand why God planned the sex experience as He did. They imply that He must have made some drastic error or used questionable judgment. This can signify only that they do not quite grasp the idea of what God's plan for two bodies uniting in love can mean.

God goes so far as to use this experience to symbolize His

love for His church. A love so intimate, so cherishing, so consummate that the best way He can describe it to us is to liken it to the beautiful relationship that He means to exist between a husband and wife. The more, then, that we cherish this sexual experience—the more beauty we see in it and constantly seek to confer on it—the more we understand His love for us. As Christ's followers, we are then bound to explore sensitively this part of our personhood and learn from Him how we might best understand His will for our sexuality. I look forward to sharing this exploration with you in the following chapters.

And Then There Is Ellen White

"Well, I know that God invented sex, but I'm not quite sure He cleared it with Ellen White!" The remark was made by a bewildered person who felt thoroughly confused over what she had been told about Mrs. White's statements on sexuality. For although many people are willing to allow that God did intend our sexuality to be a pleasurable experience as well as a spiritual happening, they do not really understand what Ellen White has to say about this component of marriage. And what is more confusing, it *is* possible to take excerpts of her written words and make them agree with antisexual biases.

This brandished material has been the means of "turning off" many people to the extent that they do not persevere in studying out the perceived contradictions for themselves; rather, they discount her completely. She is too many times seen as a tight-lipped, inhibited killjoy—too old to understand anyway.

I know that this amazing woman does not need me to defend her; but I should like, just the same, to spend some time in exploring some dimensions of what she says on this subject. My study has helped me a great deal in understanding the warm and loving things I believe her to be saying. It has also helped others whom I have talked with—people whose confusion has been great enough to endanger the sexual experience of their marriage.

Actually, most of the material Ellen White wrote on sexuality was written in the early years of her ministry, when she was a young woman. She was married when she was nineteen years of age, and her first son was born two days before her first wedding anniversary. She subsequently had three more sons, and her marriage lasted for many years.

She was writing during a time when sexuality was not a proper subject of public discussion. During much of this time Queen Victoria was lending her influence to a rather stilted, stuffy rigidity in social conduct, to the extent that the word *Victorianism* is used to suggest just that meaning. In the next chapter we will review some of the historical aspects of sexual thought, including Victorianism; but for now let us recall it as a time when sexuality was something which was thought not quite proper for a lady to enjoy, but rather for her to endure. For Ellen White to have written of it in warm and endearing terms seems rather avant garde. But then, that should not surprise us.

During this time sexuality was also fraught with many anxieties with respect to conception. Only highly unreliable and unsatisfactory modes of contraception were known. When sexual experience is connected with anxiety, the result is not beneficial. The physical condition of women was generally not as good as it is now. Because of harmful fashions, ignorance about a nourishing dietary, and less healthful living conditions women were not as vigorous and robust. Unrepaired childbirth trauma was no doubt sometimes responsible for discomfort and even pain with intercourse. And this when gentleness and understanding were not the standard mind-set for husbands. It is important to understand what the average wife was experiencing sexually to realize what Ellen White was speaking against.

In the compilation *The Adventist Home*, particularly in section V, "From the Marriage Altar," she has some very forthright things to say about some types of sexuality. And she speaks, as was her manner when deeply concerned about an issue, in a very hard-hitting, militant way. She was a crusader against whatever she saw which did not suggest God's interests were being upheld. Frequently she speaks strongly against "animal passions," "lustful passions," "carnal lust," "passions of a base quality," and "animal propensities." What did she mean by these? Obviously, she did *not* mean a blanket condemnation of sexuality, for she is already on record as saying that "the marriage relation" (a euphemism for intercourse as are "family relation" and "marriage privileges") represent the "tender and sacred union that exists between Christ and His people." And she goes on to quote Isaiah and Solomon as supporting this symbolism (Isaiah 54:4, 5; Song of Solomon 2:16; 4:7; 5:10). There is, then, a beautiful and tender demonstration of love which is worthy of such symbolism admitted in her pages.

Why not, I wonder, take these statements at face value, then? What are we talking about when we talk about "animal propensities"? My mind goes to pets we have had. Their copulation was in no way connected with a love relationship. There was no interest in pleasuring the other, no cherishing, no endearment. Participating with different partners is common in the animal world. There is sometimes a tendency to cause pain or harm to the partner—biting, scratching, seizing and holding by force. I want to state strongly that I am against that kind of sexual expression too. And so are many modern writers. Let me give you an example of a few. Harry Hollis: "Animal sex is purely seasonal, glandular, instinctual and compulsive." Clark Ellzey: "If sex is sought on the animal level, nothing but animal results can be expected." Ira Reiss: "Sex should be person-centered rather than body-centered."

Lester Kirkendall: "The quality of the interpersonal relationship is important." Alexander Lowen and Robert Levin: "When the act of sex is no longer an act of love, it is a physiological function that we have in common with other animals. . . . Sex by itself cannot yield deep and enduring satisfaction on an animal level."

Now, does that sound so much different from what Ellen White said decades ago? How can she be antisex when she is saying the same things as psychologists who by no stretch of the imagination could be considered antisex are saying today?

Whenever one or both spouses make simple tension release the primary goal of their sexual congress, when fighting and hostility instead of loving expressions precede it, when exploitation rather than tender concern is the accompaniment, I believe these to be the baser passions Ellen White speaks against.

But in contradistinction she speaks over and over again warm and wonderful things about the sexual relationship of a husband and wife in marriage. Let's look together at a few of these: "He [Jesus] looks with pleasure upon the family relationship where sacred and unselfish love bears sway."—*The Adventist Home*, p. 121. "There is a quality of love in the marriage relation which God recognizes as holy."—*Ibid.*, p. 123. "Keep the soil of the heart mellow by *manifestations* of love and affection."—*Ibid.*, p. 19. "Husbands and wives may share happiness in this union that angels of God commend."—*Ibid.*, p. 102. "All who enter into matrimonial relations with a holy purpose—the husband to obtain the pure affections of a woman's heart, the wife to soften and improve her husband's character and give it completeness—fulfill God's purpose for them."—*Ibid.*, p. 99. "Angels of God will be guests in the home, and their holy vigils will hallow the marriage chamber."—*Ibid.*, p. 94. This sounds to me as though Ellen White fully recognized the beauty which a loving sexual relationship can bring to marriage.

Some have been confused by her use of the term "abusing marriage privileges" as though it might indicate that excesses of expression were indicated. It is important for us to realize that much of the material which Ellen White wrote on this subject was compiled from what we might call "case histories"—or responding to specific situations. While some of the material is generalizable from one case to another, obviously not all of it is applicable to every marriage. It is dangerous to pick out a couple of sentences from any case history and try to form a whole framework from it. When she was writing to Mr. and Mrs. X or to Mr. Y, she indeed knew what she was talking about in speaking of their abuse of privileges. We do not know. The advice was good for them. I hope they profited by it. But this does not mean that Mr. and Mrs. Z, who are enjoying a satisfying sexual experience which meets their needs emotionally and physically, should be expected to heed the same counsel that others might benefit from.

Some years ago I heard a story attributed to a sincere Adventist minister. He was so anxious to conform his eating habits to the good counsel which Ellen White had written that when he read a statement that inferred he was eating too much, he decided to cut down and simply have a bowl of granola three times a day. After a few days of that, he read the message again; and it still said he was eating too much. So he cut down to a half a bowl of granola three times a day. After several days on this regime, imagine his surprise when he read the statement again and found it still condemning him for eating too much!

The inference is clear. The message applies to a particular person *when* appropriate. Granted, there is peril in reading constructive messages and always applying them to someone else, not realizing their relevance for us. As in many other areas of Christian living, we must use our sanctified judgment to experience balanced Christian sexuality.

Sometimes we talk to people who are sure they have read somewhere that Ellen White advocates sex for reproduction only. This was certainly true of some of her contemporaries, particularly Dr. John Kellogg. In his book *The Plain Facts About Sexual Life*, written in 1879, he purported that many evils could be avoided if intercourse were for the purpose of procreation only, stating, "There would be less sensual enjoyment but more elevated joy." However, Mrs. White did not share this view. According to an article by Ellen White's grandson Arthur in *The Ministry* of April 1969, J. N. Loughborough wrote a letter to a gentleman who was troubled over this question. He had been told that Ellen White carried this view. Elder Loughborough writes to reassure him that "Sister White has given no sanction to those who advocate that position."

Here is a portion of his letter to that gentleman, written in 1907: "One man here in California had written a tract to that effect and wanted to get her sanction to his printing it. He went down to see her, but she said that she could not see him but sent word to him that 'he had better leave that matter alone.'

"He pressed the matter and wanted to see her and finally she consented to see him. When he had finished what he had to say to her she asked him if he was through. He replied that he was and she said, 'Go home, and be a man.' He took the hint and the tract was never printed."

I propose that other evidence demonstrates that the "sex for procreation only" philosphy is in error. God made men and women to have the desire and ability to perform sexually long after the reproductive period in women is past, and this ideally to the great satisfaction of both. Unlike other animals, which have seasonal or rhythmic sexual contact, the biological reality is that humans enjoy sex through the weeks, months, and years on a continual basis.

I think it is interesting to realize that only the human species experiences orgasm per se. There is no animal duplication of this human phenomenon. This would seem to indicate that sexual union is more than a procreative act for God's human children; it is a special gift to rational beings. Also, though some animals ovulate upon sexual contact, suggesting that these two activities are coupled for that purpose, in the human female these two functions do not bear that relationship.

We spoke earlier in this chapter of Ellen White's reinforcing the biblical concept that the loving relationship between a man and his wife was symbolic of Christ's love for His church. These loving passages from the Song of Solomon were not unknown to her. The dialogue speaks words such as these:

"Let him kiss me with the kisses of his mouth—for your love is more delightful than wine." Song of Solomon 1:2, N.I.V.

"His left arm is under my head, and his right arm embraces me." Chapter 2:6.

"How delightful is your love, my sister, my bride!
How much more pleasing is your love than wine,
and the fragrance of your perfume than any spice!
Your lips drop sweetness as the honeycomb, my bride;
milk and honey are under your tongue." Chapter 4:10, 11.

"Let us go early to the vineyards to see
  if the vines have budded,
if their blossoms have opened,
  and if the pomegranates are in bloom—
there I will give you my love." Chapter 7:12.

This beautiful literature does not intimate a reluctant love experience. Sexual expression is not seen as something to be endured, begrudged, permitted, or passively borne. On the contrary, these are expressions of joyousness, delight, and eagerness. Ellen White suggests that in marriage "each is to minister to the happiness of the other."—*The Adventist Home*,

p. 103. What a beautiful demonstration of this the Song of Solomon depicts. Truly a "house with love in it, where love is expressed in words and looks and deeds" (*Ibid.*, p. 109) is consistent with the biblical philosophy and the spirit of prophecy.

I am emphasizing this because I have found it necessary many times in counseling couples to help them understand what God intended for their sexuality. I am reassured to realize that He entrusted to His servant the privilege of bringing these concepts to us in warm and loving terms.

Where do some of our negative ideas come from, then? In the next two chapters we will explore this further.

What Went Wrong?

This is an important question in view of the perfect relationship which was instituted in the Garden of Eden. As long as Adam and Eve's love and concern was for one another and their worship of God was selfless, their union was ideal. While their thoughts and desires were centered on this unity, the happiness of their marriage was not violated. Eve stood by Adam's side as his equal, "his second self"—(Ellen G. White, *Patriarchs and Prophets,* p. 46), and together they personally communed with God each day.

Now from this point let's take a walk through history—a necessarily brief one—and try to recognize the influences from different historical periods which still reach down to affect the human sexual response. Beginning with the garden experience of idyllic bliss, we come to a time when self-serving thoughts took the place of a couple's faithfulness to one another and to God. It usually follows that when man thinks he has a better plan for his life than God has, unhappiness follows. One of the first results of this primal couple's disobedience to God's test was the secondary role that Eve must now take. When the discordant note of sin entered Eden, the harmonious relationship could no longer be maintained on the basis of complete equality—sin does not naturally result in peace, trust, and cooperation. Ellen White states that the new configuration of their roles could "have proved a blessing to them; but man's abuse of the supremacy thus given him has too often rendered the lot of women very bitter and made her life a burden."—*Ibid.*, p. 59.

This "bitter lot of women" began early and became well integrated with sexual dysfunctionality. When women are perceived and treated as inferior beings, it paves the way for exploitation and degeneracy. The male then becomes the aggressor, the perpetrator, functioning in a way inconsistent with the cherishing, the caring, and the concern that is part of a loving sexual relationship.

Though respect for women among the ancient Hebrews was certainly on a higher plane than in the nations about them, certain practices militated against experiencing sexuality in a true climate of loving concern. These would include regarding women as property, ascribing them less value than males—a double standard of marital fidelity and easy divorce. Copying the customs of nations about them, the Hebrews introduced plural marriages and the taking of concubines. This practice resulted in disharmony in families. Sexual pleasure was seen as something to be enjoyed for its own sake; however, a heterosexual monogomous marriage was acknowledged as God's ideal. Unfaithfulness to marriage vows was theoretically proscribed. These precepts remained even though the people of Israel frequently deviated from them. Another aspect which deserves our notice is the openness and frankness with which sexuality was treated in this culture. The Bible gives no evidence of hidden, restricted handling of these topics. This came much later.

Neither Roman nor Greek civilizations provided an atmosphere that elevated the marital union. The Greek statesman, Demosthenes, (3000 B.C.) indicated that it might take several of this lesser order of being—women—to take care of man's needs: "Mistresses we keep for pleasure, concubines for daily attendance upon our person, wives to bear us legitimate children and be our faithful housekeepers." The wife could be repudiated and simply dismissed for barrenness or even if her husband found her unattractive or uncongenial. Ancient Greeks considered man by nature to be bisexual. In addition to wives and concubines, the well-to-do Greek patron frequently had a young male as a homosexual companion. This was socially acceptable and indeed sometimes encouraged. Solon, the Greek lawgiver, gave powerful civil rights to those who practiced homosexuality. This life-style was not limited to men. In fact we derive the term "Lesbian" from certain women residents of the Isle of Lesbos in the Aegean Sea. These women were sexual companions to one another.

Turning now to early Roman times, we find that a strictly monogamous society changed when successful wars and accumulated wealth seemed to pave the way for a more decadent life-style. The inferior status of women was continued. Third century B.C. Roman statesman Cato stated; "If you were to catch your wife in adultery, you would kill her with impunity without trial; but if she were to catch you, she could not dare to lay a finger upon you." A husband had the right to inflict "moderate chastisement," that is, he could "beat her violently with whips and sticks, but not knock her down with an iron bar."

Goodsell in his book *A History of Marriage and the Family* records that imperial Roman society was corrupt and degenerate, with great laxity in sexual relationships. He states that the drinking, gluttony, brutalizing games and exhibitions of all sorts served "the ends of arousing animal passions which, in court circles at least, not unfrequently sought outlets in unrestrained sexual license." All of this caused Juvenal, a first-century A.D. poet, to lament, "Chastity has long since left the earth."

Christ's thirty-year first-advent ministry to this world was carried on in this setting. What a contrast His life, example, and ideas presented! His ministry included special consideration for women. He attempted to raise the status of women, and years later, in the time of the early Christian church, His efforts finally proved successful. Some women were able to occupy very prominent and honorable positions. This was also true in ancient Israel, to some extent.

Christ's work was sensitive to the human needs of all, whether it was feeding hungry crowds, relieving physical suffering, or avoiding family embarrassment at a wedding reception. His pronounced aim was to give abundant life to all, and this included dignifying and restating the stability and quality of marital relationships. He honored marriage and emphasized its permanence by restricting the ease with which divorce was available. He also broadened the base of marital unfaithfulness from a narrow interpretation of the deed to attitudinal infidelity which precedes the act, in the mind and heart.

Following this time, in the second and third centuries, a very important concept became prevalent in the Christian church; and it had far-reaching affects on sexual behavior. This was the dichotomizing of things of the spirit and things of the flesh. It followed, then, that all expressions of body pleasures—including sexual expression—were thought to be evil. Adam's expulsion from the Garden of Eden was seen by some as a result of sexual sin, Eve being seen as the temptress. Tertullian, an early church father, accused women in this vein: "You are the devil's gateway. You are the unsealer of the forbidden tree. You are the first deserter of the divine law. You are she who pursuaded him [Adam] who the devil was not valiant enough to attack. You destroyed so easily God's image, man. As a dangerous seducer of men, let woman seclude herself, dress in sober garments, veil her face, and walk humbly in the earth."

Sexual expression was seen as a contaminating process. To perform the sex act for pleasure was accounted sinful. The church theologians warned Christians that the Holy Spirit left the chambers while married couples carried on sexual intercourse, even though the couple desired pregnancy. Since marriage then was seen as contributing to moral turpitude, the church refused to perform this ceremony on certain sacred days of the year. A wife's duty was to discourage her husband's sexual interest, even kissing. The most highly revered people were those who would become celibate and deny themselves the "pleasures of the flesh."

Some of these concepts have carried through to the present. Their influence has been the more impressive because of their churchly origin. Many people are influenced by these early sentiments without realizing their beginning. But when loving sexual expression in marriage is seen as disgusting, as nasty, as repulsive, as offensive, or as dirty, something is amiss. These attitudes cannot be used to describe an act which God created and blessed. The status of women was pulled even lower; for now women were seen not only as inferior, but as a corrupting influence. Chrysostom, an early Greek church father, declared, "A woman is a necessary evil, a natural temptation, a desirable calamity, a domestic peril, a deadly fascination, and a painted ill." How many centuries will be needed to erase completely the results of such thinking on the consciousness of both men and women we cannot yet know.

We will now pass on to the Middle Ages, where there is seen some backlash to the prior inhibited expression of sexuality. Adultery was a "social diversion" according to Lewishohn (*A History of Sexual Customs*). Prostitution flourished, as did rape and incest, particularly among the nobility and royalty. Alcuin, an advisor to Charlemagne, observed that the count was "absolutely submerged under a flood of fornication, adultery, and incest." In King Arthur's court, the legend reports a magic mantle was produced to be worn only by a chaste female. The record states that there was not one lady present able to wear it.

Boniface, an English monk, observed that the English "utterly despised matrimony . . . [and] utterly refused to have legitimate wives and continued to live in lechery and adultery after the manner of neighing horses and braying asses."

If one good thing might be said about sexuality in this era, it would be that women and men at least saw sexuality to be an enjoyable experience, "more for delight than to multiply." So one extreme, asceticism, was countered by another, promiscuity. God's ideal of marriage suffered at the hands of both.

The Reformation, of the sixteenth century, greatly strengthened marriage. With great strides in religious thinking, human alliances were enhanced. Women's status began to rise somewhat as education in languages and classics began to be available to them. Books were written in their defense, and men began to look at them through different eyes.

There was an interesting difference in the viewpoints of two great reformers—Calvin and Luther. Calvin lost his wife and only child soon after marriage. He failed to use his influence to raise significantly the depressed status of women. He also portrayed sexual intercourse in marriage as a joyless activity whose sacredness was suspect.

Luther, on the other hand, was happily married to a former nun, Katherine von Bora. They parented six children. Luther found it not indecent or immodest to write openly on sexual matters. His famous little rhyme has often been quoted by both men and women as a statement supporting their feelings on how often a couple should have sexual intercourse in marriage. His oft-quoted advice reads:

A week two
Is women's due
Harms neither me nor you
makes in a year twice fifty two

While women were seen as capable of sexual desire, they were still perceived as persons who ministered to the comforts and needs of their husbands, to the exclusion of their own needs—while husbands were not expected to reciprocate in kind.

Hand in hand with the Reformation went the Renaissance, introducing a change in the worlds of science and art. Women still had little confidence in their creative ability, however, for few were allowed to become eminent in any field. Marriage did not advance to become a humanistic concern. It was seen mainly as a convenient arrangement for legitimizing children and advancing the financial and social status of persons involved. It was not considered to be a relationship of tenderness and caring. Romantic love was not associated with marriage. In the minds of many it was unwise to mingle love and marriage, for that might bring "disasters, or at least certain disappointments." An unnamed sixteenth-century French writer suggested that a wife existed to "pay honor, reverence, and respect to her husband as to her master and sovereign lord, obedience in all things, just and lawful, adapting herself and bending to the habits and disposition of her husband like the useful mirror which faithfully reflects the face, having no private purpose, love, or thought." A wife was thought of as a naïve, childlike creation who, "good or bad, needs the stick."

English writer Lord Chesterfield, in a letter to his son, states about women, "A man of sense only trifles with them. . . . No flattering is either too high or too low for them; they will greedily follow the highest and accept the lowest." Shakespeare, through the character Katherine in *The Taming of the Shrew*, says, "I am ashamed that women are so simple." Simplified marriage laws of the time were often misused to exploit women, who were enjoined to feign ignorance and close their eyes to their husband's dalliances, but remain chaste themselves. Rousseau, French philosopher of the sixteenth century, stated: "The education of women should always be relative to that of men. To please, to take care of us when grown up, to advise, to console, to render our lives easy and agreeable; these are the duties of women at all times, and what they should be taught in their infancy."

How easy to trace through these erstwhile thoughts the self-depreciatory feelings so many contempory women have about themselves. Only in recent decades have women been self-confident enough to enter professional areas of interest, in any numbers. In consideration of centuries of abuse, then, perhaps they may be excused if sometimes their manner of gaining recognition may seem innappropriate or strident.

These European influences we have explored were felt also in young America. In colonial families, insanity in women was sometimes thought to be the result of women actively pursuing such liberal arts as reading and writing books—activities too taxing for their limited intellects. It was felt, records Steward Queen in *The Family in Various Cultures,* that women should stay home and attend their household affairs.

American statesman Calhoun is credited with feeling that women were "instruments of male gratification," and indicated that male gratification was a "vicarious sacrifice to the peopling of the continent." A rather curious concept was reported in the *Lady's Magazine,* August 1771: "Licentious commune between the sexes . . . may be carried on by men without contaminating the mind, so as to render them unworthy of the marriage bed and incapable of discharging the virtuous and honorable duties of the husband, father, and friend. . . . [but] the contamination of the female mind is a necessary and inseparable consequence of illicit intercourse with men. . . . Women are universally virtuous, or utterly undone." Expression of feeling was commonly restrained and formal. For example, an interesting footnote to history informs us that in New England a sea captain was severely punished for publicly kissing his wife on Sunday, just after having returned from a long sea journey.

Queen Victoria's influence on the social values of her time are as considerable as her influence in other areas. There was a reversion to the idea that enjoying sex was a morally suspect undertaking. No nice or decent girl was to admit enjoying her sexuality. She should help her husband enjoy the sensualness of the act as little as possible while still allowing him to father her children. Queen Victoria herself referred to the sex act in a letter to her daughter as "something that we poor women must go through."

Since sex was not seen as a sanctioned experience, it was thought to be better to restrict it as much as possible. Even love poems were looked on askance. The Bible was considered a "dangerous book to fall into the hands of anyone with an unchaste mind." The extremes to which this excessive restriction was carried are shown by the discouragement of regular washing of the body, particularly the genital parts, since this might inspire impure thoughts and lead to impure acts. Voluptuously carved piano legs were sometimes draped with cloth pantaloons for decency's sake. Books by male and female authors were, by some householders, segregated on the shelves. Sometimes cages were employed to fit over boys' genitals at night. These contraptions were carefully locked to prevent masturbation. And some of these implements even sported spikes sticking out of them to make mastrubation even less likely. Thinking sexual thoughts was held to demean women, but not necessarily men.

How much of this thinking is still prevelent now we cannot estimate; but when a woman says, "Sex is only for a man's enjoyment, and I do try to please my husband"—she is not far from Victorianism. When a modern Eve reads Ellen White's caution to a specific person in a case study as a blanket condemnation of marital sex, she is reflecting cultural, not spiritual, values. And when a man makes a demand upon his wife in an unloving manner and castigates her for not giving him his "rights," he displays an attitude reminiscent of that same time.

In the last century or so women have succeeded in upgrading their status. These changes have come slowly, and women have not yet arrived at full equality. However, women have come into a role which now admits that their needs and desires for sexuality are biologically, not merely culturally, ordained.

Certain discoveries and inventions played a part in changing sexual experience. One of these was the condom, which came into use at the end of the nineteenth century. Occlusive pessaries, diaphragms, and various vaginal suppositories also were employed, though in a more limited way, for contraception. These contributed to sexual experiences less fraught with fear of pregnancy. The automobile provided a space for a man and a woman to find privacy for lovemaking, prompting the cartoon comment, "The parlor takes wheels."

Because of a woman's continuing lack of opportunity to be as independent as a man, marriage was a status which held security for her. Therefore, young ladies were generally eager for matrimony regardless of whether desires of love preceded it or not. An elaborate system of games was sometimes outlined for young girls in a number of publications of the day. Gambits proposed to young ladies included teasing and trickery designed to culminate in "capturing the young man of her choice." Only in the last decade or so have women's magazines modified their presentation of ways to catch men's attention, ways to be husband-pleasers, "even to what seems a sacrifice of their own identity." Certainly a time of greater honesty is a harbinger of better things to come.

Dr. Van de Velde, in his book *The Ideal Marriage*, published in 1926, was one of the first physicians to give advice which included a husband's part in doing something to bring his wife sexual pleasure. His book is still interesting and profitable reading. In the language quaintly reminiscent of the time, he suggested, "In any erotic play executed with delicate reverence and consideration, and above all, when lovers have not become accustomed and attuned, a considerable amount of time should be given to kisses and manual caresses before the genitals are touched. After gentle stroking and clasping of the accessory organs the hand should lightly and timidly brush the abdomen, the mons-pubis, the inner side of the thighs, alight swiftly on the sexual organs and pass swiftly to the other side. Only by a cautious and circuitous route should it approach the holy place of sex and tenderly seek admittance."

This unusual man realized the multiplicity of factors which enhance intercourse. He felt that it was important for a woman's enjoyment that there be "a conscious intention to enjoy all the stimuli received."—*Ibid.*, p. 176. He also realized the importance of a young unmarried woman having an adequate physical examination to check sexual organs for defects. We might not sympathize with the doctor's advice in procuring this information. He suggested that the parents arrange for the doctor to give the physical examination by falsely claiming that it was intended for an insurance policy! But this does give some indication of how difficult it was for a young woman to submit to examination of a part of her body which was so disparaged. Modern women still have feelings akin to hers.

Our walk through history now brings us to the present. We have highlighted many of our attitudes and ideas—both negative and positive—that we owe to past centuries. In the next chapter we can begin to discover the ideas which delay and sometimes even prevent our sexual experience from being as significant an expression of love as it might be.

A Lifetime of Influences

Unbelievable as it may seem to some, prenatal influences are important in determing a person's life adjustments. Aside from the obvious effects on an unborn child of the mother's general health, her diet and exercise, the matter of her *emotional* well-being is also consequential.

Ellen White has counseled: "If before the birth of her child she is self-indulgent, if she is selfish, impatient, and exacting, these traits will be reflected in the disposition of the child. . . .

"But if the mother unswervingly adheres to right principles, if she is temperate and self-denying, if she is kind, gentle, and unselfish, she may give her child these same precious traits of character."—*The Ministry of Healing*, pp. 372, 373.

A contemporary theoretician, Dr. Warren Gadpaille, states, "Even the mother's emotional states and attitudes which will deeply affect her baby after it is born, cannot make themselves felt only through a biological channel. . . . There can be no question that a mother's emotional states can be communicated to the fetus that she is carrying. Many if not all emotions are reflected in changes in blood-borne hormones and other chemicals which can cross through the placenta into the bloodstream of the fetus. Stress in particular produces body chemistry changes which, if sustained, ultimately alter and disorder many vital functions."—*The Cycles of Sex.* (Charles Scribner's Sons: NY, 1976.)

How can all of this have any bearing on future sexual enjoyment? Anything which tends to enhance the general health has a positive affect on sexuality. The gift of vitality, of a calm and inner harmony, cannot be valueless in future experiences.

Infancy can be a very significant factor in future sexual patterns. As the child is fed and kept clean and warm in the routine of a good mother-child relationship, the baby builds confidence in her or his environment. Even a very thin baby learns that she or he can summon attention when a need is felt. This gives feelings of security and trust if consistently experienced. These feelings of assurance which the infant comes to depend on are further enhanced if the caring for is enriched by gentleness, loving handling, and soothing voices.

Most people are acquainted with the study done by Harlow in which tiny, newborn monkeys were separated into groups for different types of care. One group had all of the biological needs met, but in a setting devoid of softness, handling, or attention. The food came from a mechanical, utilitarian arrangement which held the bottle for nursing but provided no softness, good body feelings, or personal care taking. Another group had a "cloth mother," a soft padded structure which held the bottle and provided some creature comforts. The result of this experiment, among other things, demonstrated that the babies with no comfort were frightened and insecure and were unable to learn how to relate lovingly to others. This included the inability to later engage in mating activities. Here is indicated the very early need for a baby to feel consistently loved and cherished by caressing, touching, rubbing, snuggling, and all of the other warm and wonderful things that send positive messages through the skin. Further, when this is accompanied by talking, cooing, singing, and mellow-sounding nonsense syllables, a baby—from the very first—enjoys a sense of belonging, of being loved. What a precious heritage such a baby has.

To many it would seem that *baby* is a sexually neutral word and and that there is little difference in the treatment of boy and girl babies. This does not appear to be the case. Observation has indicated that even in the nursery the boys receive a different kind of attention from that received by the girls. Girls more often hear soft baby talk and are treated more as cuddly, fragile, and delicate. Boys, on the other hand, more often hear language like this: "Isn't he a big boy! He's going to be a real man!" This language is characterized by different voice tones and different body language. A baby boy is already evaluated for his greater size, strength, and alertness—as though this increases his acceptability.

I think that little girls have an advantage at this stage by receiving more gentle treatment, with no demands to be anything more than pink and adorable. Little boys seem to "measure up" better if they are bigger, stronger, and able to hold their heads up sooner. I wonder if the pattern of feeling a need to prove their masculinity carries from this stage onward. This does not seem to me to be fair or wise. May not this be a precursor of the eventual pressure that men feel to perform "sexually" in ways that they have been made to feel that the culture expects? But I am digressing. Let's get back to our infants!

By the time a child is two years old, several important things have already begun to happen. Little boys are being made aware that girls—that other kind of person—are treated differently: "You don't hit a girl." "Little boys don't cry." "Little girls go first." This seems to be giving the message that girls have a different status, are set apart, or have some advantages!

By now, also, inquisitive tiny fingers have examined their soft, cuddly selves. Something surprising might happen here—at least it may well puzzle small ones. When they find their nose, their ears, their tongue, parents smile on them benignly. But let their small digits discover the genital part of their bodies, and the result is generally anxiety and unease manifested by a frown, a quick and decided removal of the hand, or even a slap with a severe "No!" or "Nasty!" Couple this with the expression on mother's face when she changes the diaper and makes a grimace or negative sound as she removes the "offending" square. Daily repetitions of the rite cannot but give the impression that something about the genital area of the body is quite negative. Such parental reactions can affect how persons later respond to the genital area; and they help to explain why it is so often thought to be dirty, shameful, repulsive, or in a descriptive word I have heard used by young women, "yucky."

When a small lad learns to direct his urinary stream by holding his penis, he is roundly praised. Mommy and daddy both assure him that he has exhibited a fine piece of marksmanship and deserves approval. For this and many other reasons, little boys learn to be proud of their penises and think of them in very positive terms. I have not found this feeling to be one that women share about their own genitals. What God saw as "very good" when He passed judgement on His creation is somehow mentally restricted by many people to the upper parts of their bodies. I sometimes wonder how He feels about that.

Certainly now, it will not be long until the little ones perceive differences in the male and female body through observing their brothers and sisters and other relatives and friends. Now, it is gratifying to note to what lengths some parents will go to answer carefully all of their child's questions. Well, almost all. When this child points to an animal, a machine, or a toy and asks, "What's that?" parents lovingly and carefully explain in words that a little one can understand. But when asked about the difference of anatomy between a boy and a girl, the curiosity is rewarded by embarrasment, deviousness, distracting techniques, or just plain ignoring. Part of this I believe to be because few parents have any comfort with the words that apply to the genital parts.

This is not surprising, since they probably grew up using quaint euphemisms rather than the correct words for body parts or body excretory functions. What a wondrous list of simple repetitive syllables have been known to call to mind these concepts! Should it surprise us, then, when children giggle and titter or feel an elated excitment when they hear the correct words for something that mom and dad have indicated is too mysterious, too questionable, too emotion laden to be forthright about?

Soon enough come questions which indicate a desire to know what life is all about. Or, put more simply by little ones, "Where do babies come from?" Does not an inquisitive little mind deserve a more truthful answer than "The cabbage patch," "The doctor brings it," or even "I'll tell you when you get older"? The answers to such questions can have a negative or positive effect on the child's understanding of the beauties of God's divine plan for sexuality.

Another area of concern for a parent is the play that they sometimes find their children engaged in either with siblings or neighbors. Frequently it is considerably less emotion packed for the child than it is for the parent. It is not surprising that children should be interested in "playing house" or visiting the "doctor." It may easily be misinterpreted by parents who came upon the scene, finding their offspring in surprising situations. The surest way to make this activity go "underground" is to scream, yell, cry, threaten, or scold. Far better to sit down and let the children explain to you what they are doing and what the meaning of their play is. You may decide that your children are innocent of anything sinister or corrupt. You may realize that you have not provided enough nondirective supervision in the play time or taken enough time to play with them. Perhaps simply boredom has lead them into activity which concerns you. It is not impossible that some types of sexual play could cause physical and emotional trauma. But so can overreaction. As in most other areas of child rearing, problems are better handled after a cooling-off period, in a calm and explanatory—rather than an excited and denunciatory—frame of mind.

Sometimes parents are deeply concerned because their child has come upon them in some part of lovemaking. I believe that a child has a right to be oblivious to the most intimate details of their parents' private love-exchange. What goes on is impossible for a young child to understand. It does not always look or even sometimes sound particularly loving to the child. I encourage parents to have a lock on their bedroom door—high enough so that pairs of little hands cannot reach it and run the risk of of locking themselves into that bedroom. The very explanation of why the door is sometimes closed to them can provide an excellent opportunity to talk about the special love that goes on between mommies and daddies.

When a child is school bound, significant influences multiply. New peers provide considerable input into the thinking in all areas. Sharing bathroom facilities, the child will inevitably hear discussions including words and phrases that are new, sometimes with gestures and facial expressions as well as voice tones which titillate and intrigue. All of these now accumulate in the child's awareness. If this child has found his parents unabashed when confronted with questions of any sort, it would be natural to bring these new bits and pieces of information home for discussion. What a precious opportunity then for parents and child to sort out the truth from the trash. But a child is not so likely to allow this if he has formerly had messages indicating embarrassment, shock, and disgust when sexual topics arise. It will not be necessary to "shake in your boots" when puberty nears if good communication has paved the way through the years.

And it will come! Hopefully by now both boys and girls will have been made aware of what physical body changes and what biological changes to expect. What a tragedy for a young girl to be confronted with menses or a young boy with nocturnal emissions without foreknowledge. Yet counseling experience reveals that this is too often the case. I plead with all parents of young children not to let this happen to their precious heritage. When we tell our children about what God planned for their sexuality, we are not talking about something shameful, ugly, or evil. The young do not deserve to have it seem so.

Let's talk first about menstruation. This amazing phenomenon has usually received a bad press. For centuries it has carried with it implications of shame, horror, and isolation. Menstruating women have been thought to possess evil powers and even to be capable of instigating public dangers. Pliny's history, in first century Rome, attributes to menstruating females the power to blight crops, blast gardens, kill seedlings, bring down fruit trees, kill bees, cause mares to miscarry, turn milk sour, and turn wine to vinegar. That's quite a load! Girls are now faced with a monthly event that restricts, embarrasses, and inconveniences. They are enjoined not to show, to bulge, to stain, and most of all not to omit! How girls experience their first menstruation may set precedence for future feelings about this function. Sometimes a big fuss is made over it, and a young girl is pampered and allowed to use this as a cop-out for school or tasks around home. I am not inferring that there are not sometimes unusual problems with beginning to menstruate. I am trying to make the point that when this function is treated with less anxiety and worry, it generally follows that girls can take it in their stride. I feel uncomfortable when I hear the words "the curse," "being sick," and other such phrases to denote this period. I wonder if this does not encourage a mind-set which is negative. Improper and scanty information is also something that concerns me. Some girls have told me that their whole education process on the matter of their menstruation was obtained in one line. Here is an example: "This is how to use a sanitary napkin; now don't do anything silly with the boys." Another: "The bad blood has to go somewhere." And another: "It's getting the nasty out of you." What a mockery of God's design!

Now while it is good to have a biological, matter-of-fact explanation of menstruation, I wonder if we can't do even better. This rite of passage can be seen as a proud milestone in a girl's life. She now has an even closer relationship with her mother as they share this common experience. I recall one young woman telling me that her mother had prepared her with this kind of approach. When in the middle of the night she discovered that she had evidence of the menarche, she awakened her mother with the exciting news, and these two women embraced in the night. What a glorious initiation into womanhood! Another shared with me something truly beautiful. When her mother told her father the exciting news of her "coming of age," he feted his daughter with a bouquet of red roses. These examples glorify God's plan rather than demean it.

A young boy also needs to realize what is involved when he notes evidence of nocturnal emission—"a wet dream." Before this he will most certainly have had an erection whether his parents have noticed it or not. If, having noted it earlier, they had not made an occasion to explain the meaning of his new feelings and body responses, it certainly must be done at the time his first nocturnal emissions are noted. How this is carried out, again, can bring messages of shame, guilt, and badness. As parents should know, an erection is not a willed reaction; it happens normally and naturally. Satan's planning did not design the occurence. Young boys need to realize that a nocturnal emission has been provided to take care of sexual feelings which they are not yet ready to act upon in a mature way. Nature just automatically helps to keep things comfortable for them. Nocturnal emissions should in no way be related, in their thinking, to masturbation. Some young men have felt great trauma and guilt when they have had dire warnings about masturbation and believe that nocturnal emissions—when they occur—are indeed masturbatory experiences. Again, open and forthright communication from early in life can prevent many needless worries.

We have spent some time reviewing early life experience which affects how sexuality is responded to in later years. In a later chapter we will look again at some aspects of sexuality for teenagers. But let me add here that I believe that parents, by their sensitive understanding of the sexual impulses which flood pubescent youth, can be very supportive of their children. Occasionally, we find parents who have become somewhat intimidated by their developing young people. Parents who earlier felt comfortable expressing warm and loving feelings to their children—not only verbally but in hugs and kisses—now feel inhibited. This cuts off teenagers from receiving physical affection from appropriate sources and must sometimes be confusing to them.

Again, parents are heard to tease their daughters and sons about their newly developed sexual attributes. This generally does not endear parents to their children! While the young people appreciate the sincere acknowledgment of their parents' pride in their growth and development, they are sufficiently insecure and ill at ease with their new bodies to dislike jesting or even gentle ridicule. How much better, too, if they do not hear innuendos and borderline jokes about sexuality.

Young adults have a number of choices to make in the area of their sexuality. They will decide whether marriage is the social vehicle in which they wish to meet their needs and goals. If they opt for marriage, they will make decisions as to whether parenting is a way in which they wish to express their sexuality. In terms of remaining single or marrying and having or not having children, I feel glad that young people currently are being allowed to make more choices in this regard. Several decades ago anyone who did not wish to marry, or who, being married, omitted parenting was seen as abnormal or deviant. Perhaps we are now willing to grant that a fulfilled life, marked with productivity and satisfaction, can be lived by people who are not involved in marriage and/or parenthood. A single person's choice involves sublimation of sexual activity; but that does not mean sublimation of sexuality—a quality which includes, warmth, compassion, openness, and/or arousal of the senses in enjoyment of aesthetic activities.

When a couple does make a decision for parenthood, they need to be aware that each child presents a special crisis for a marriage. Children do not invariably bless marriages. They are good indication that they can even be a disruptive factor in a marriage which is not stable. To expect an addition to a troubled marriage to heal dysfunction is not only unreasonable but it is tragic. It is best for two grown adults to work through their problems before they decide to parent. Becoming parents may indeed, if a couple is not sensitive to the possibility, create a disengagement which may usurp the primary love relationship between two people whose marriage may have at least been functional—if not glorious. A husband and wife must deliberately organize their life together so that they can maintain a sense of belonging and caring. A good sexual relationship can enhance married life throughout its years, and parenthood should interfere with it as little as possible. If it is allowed to languish during the hustle and bustle of child rearing, it is sometimes difficult to become wholly involved again in an emotionally and physically intimate relationship when the "nest is emptied." Sometimes the parents seem to one another as strangers who have been bound together only by the needs of their children. The divorce rate for this age group is rising alarmingly at this time, and perhaps this helps to explain this distressing statistic.

Couples in these years need to give loving thought and attention to plan private time alone together for sexual expression. It should be their studied intent to refuse to let extreme fatigue or preoccupation undermine their sexual bond. A spirit of joyousness and delight can pervade their private time together.

Nor need the last years of life be less blessed by the closeness and tenderness of this intimate part of marital interaction. The "humor" often associated with sexuality in the aging I feel to be entirely inappropriate—and sometimes even harmful. When older folk get the impression that their sexual interest in one another is untimely or improper, many of them are made to feel guilty or, at the least foolish. They are thus robbed of a means of expressing their love for one another.

We have taken a limited look at what sexuality can mean in all stages of the life process. We have seen how pervasive this part of our being is at each stage of life. How could it be different when our maleness and femaleness is the very means by which we are defined? In the next chapter we will deal specifically with being female and being male.

Wonderfully Made

How little we know about these wondrous "temples" which we are. Each exploration into the structure and working of our bodies leads always to further intricacies and deeper mysteries. We take for granted the smooth orderliness of our body functions, until our ignorance trips us up. Lack of correct knowledge then frequently shows up in illness and dysfunction.

In one of his psalms David demonstrates an interest in man's biological complexities: "I will praise thee; for I am fearfully and wonderfully made: marvellous are thy works; and that my soul knoweth right well. My substance was not hid from thee, when I was made in secret, and curiously wrought in the lowest parts of the earth. Thine eyes did see my substance, yet being unperfect; and in thy book all my members were written, which in continuance were fashioned, when as yet there was none of them. How precious also are thy thoughts unto me, O God! how great is the sum of them!" Psalm 139:14-17.

David's appreciation of his physical being was profound. How delightfully he presented the picture of the miraculous progression from an apparent nothingness, which then goes through a process "curiously wrought" and is fashioned into a wonderfully made body. One can sense the Holy Spirit's inspiration in these verses, when there was little, if any appreciation of the histological aspects of pre-birth growth. To see a newborn baby in its perfection and to realize that this small being can grow to be a person of stature, strength, and efficiency is to be aware of a truly miraculous process. To be indifferent to learning all one can about this process seems, at the least negligent.

Some very pointed remarks come to us through Ellen White with reference to the necessity of being well informed about our physical selves. Note this one: "All need to become acquainted with that most wonderful of all organisms, the human body. They should understand the functions of the various organs and the dependence of one upon another for the healthy action of all."—*The Ministry of Healing*, p. 128.

We could fill this entire chapter with instruction from the same pen which may vary in words, but not in meaning. I have noted that the enthusiastic assent to this admonition can stop abruptly when reference is made to our need for knowledge about the sexual parts of our anatomy and the physiology which describes how they function. That seems to me to be an echo again of the past attitude which considered the sexuality of our bodies as depraved and shameful. I do not find a disclaimer in Ellen White's instruction which denounces the study of some parts of our bodies while other areas of study are to be vigorously pursued.

I cannot leave this area without calling attention to two more comments by Ellen White: "As the mechanism of the body is studied, attention should be directed to its wonderful adaptation of means to ends, the harmonious action and dependence of the various organs."—*Education*, p. 198.

"The laws that govern our physical organism, God has written upon every nerve, muscle, and fiber of the body."—*Ibid.*, p. 196.

At the risk of belaboring the point, I again wish to emphasize that God's imprint is on each part of the body. A faithfulness to the sexual body responses which He ordained must not be seen as a runaway, perverted digression from His plan. He designed sexuality in its tiniest detail as an emotional-physical expression of love.

At this point we will look at the physical aspects of our sexuality. While we will not be able to go into this in great detail, at least it will give us a stepping-off place as we begin discussing the process of sexuality. This cannot be done effectively without use of diagrams for reference in the textual material. Now if you find yourself rushing to close the book if someone comes into the room or if you want to hide these pages from your children, stop a moment. This reflex action may be an indication to you of your attitude toward part of God's creation—which may be negatively oriented, shrouded with mystery too great to explore, or even simply that it is too uncomfortable to discuss. My hope is that, in bringing this material to you, each of these above conditions may be ameliorated. My dearest wish is that you may be able to discuss comfortably this bonding component designed for you and your spouse with her or him, and that appropriate helpful dialogue between you and your children will be the basis of enhancing and spiritualizing sexuality in your family.

From the moment that the sperm cells, which have found their way from the vaginal canal to the fallopian tube, meets the monthly ovum (egg), which has followed its course from the ovary to the entrance of the same tubes, these sperms begin to try to penetrate the surface of the egg. If one of these active sperms succeeds, it carries with it the potentional chromosomes which will join with those from the mother contained in the egg. At that time the fertilized cell begins its miraculous process of growth. The biological program has already determined the sex of the child and its bodily characteristics such as build, coloring, constitution, etc. Within the first few weeks cell structures already are differentiating the physical features of a male and a female embryo. God's plan for sexual maturity carries on through hormonal changes at puberty until a young adult becomes ready for sexual experience.

Certain parts of the body are considered erogenous zones. That simply means that these parts of the body were designed to contain nerve receptors which have the potentional for arousing sexual desire when stimulated. Some of these erogenous zones are genitally situated, and some are not. In either the female or male, the latter could include the face, mouth, ears, neck, eyelids, shoulders, breasts, lower abdomen, buttocks, and thighs, particularly the inner portions. There is much individual variation in the feeling derived from stimulation of these areas. Generally, a light touch is more pleasing than a firm or brisk approach.

The female genital area consists of mons veneris (hair-covered mound), labia majora and minora (sometimes called outer and inner lips), the clitoris, and the vagina. Sometimes the entire region is known as the vulva, or vulvar area. The part separating the vagina and the anus is known as the fourchette; the whole area including the vulva, fourchette, and the anus is known as the perineum. A look at the diagram will help you to understand the position of these parts of the genital area. Another diagram will show you how they fit together internally.

In noting the male genitalia, we find again how wonderfully adaptive these organs are for their role in sexual union with their female counterparts. Included are the penis, which consists of the glans, or the very sensitive area on the head of the penis, the corona—or ring—which makes a ridge between the head and the rest of the penis—and the main body of the penis, known as the shaft. Lying behind and beneath the penis is the scrotum. Beginning on the underside of the scrotum, between the testicles, is a line which carries around the frontal surface

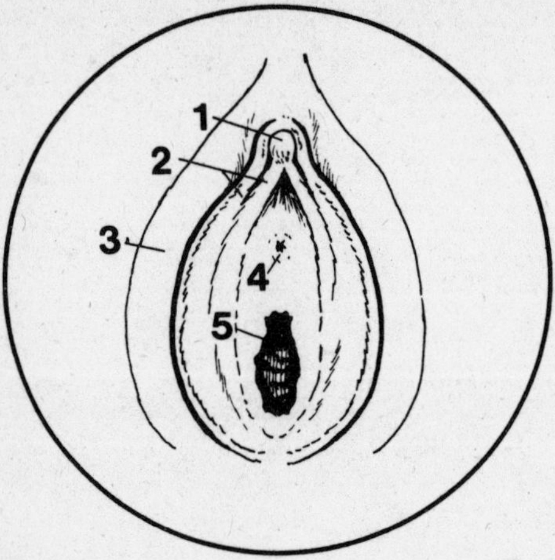
1
2
3
4
5

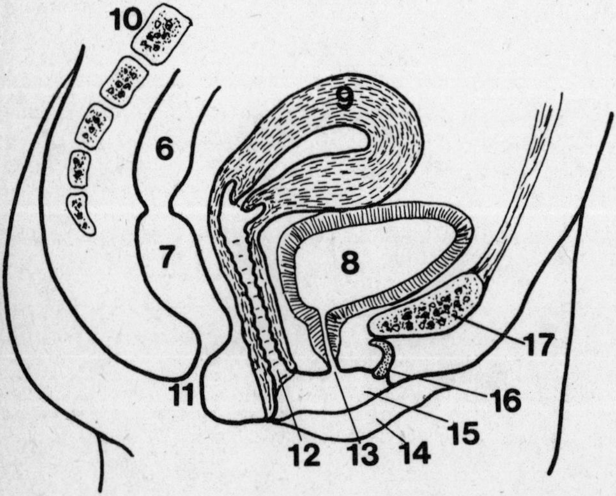
10
9
6
7
8
17
11
16
15
12
13
14

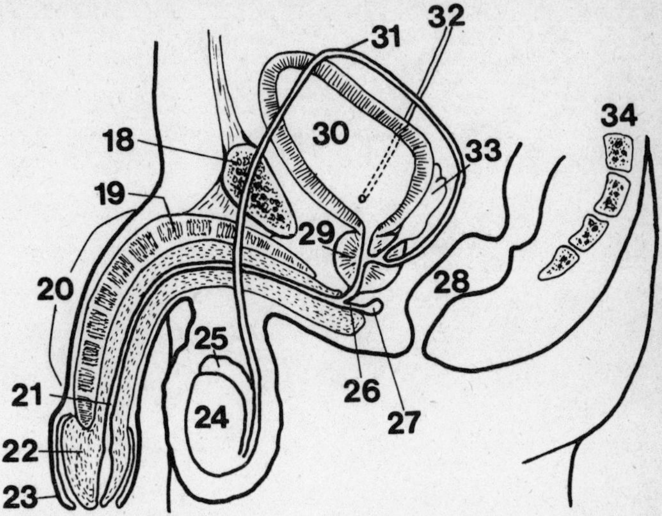

FEMALE

1. clitoris
2. labium minor
3. labium major
4. urethral orifice
5. vaginal orifice
6. sigmoid colon
7. rectum
8. bladder
9. uterus
10. vertebral column
11. anus
12. vagina
13. urethra
14. labium major
15. labium minor
16. clitoris
17. pubic symphysis

MALE

18. pubic symphysis
19. corpus cavernosum
20. shaft
21. urethra
22. glans penis
23. prepuce (foreskin)
24. testicle
25. epididymis
26. ejaculatory duct
27. bulbourethral gland
28. rectum
29. prostate gland
30. bladder
31. vas deferens
32. ureter
33. seminal vesicle
34. vertebral column

of the scrotum, and continues on the back or inner surface of the penis to the corona. This is known as the frenulum and is a very sensitive area.

Now we have established the terminology which will be used throughout the rest of these chapters. For some it may seem a strange and forbidding language. But I believe if we are to study the "mechanics" of these magnificent body temples of ours, if we are to understand its "wonderful adaptation of means to ends," we must do so with intelligence and understanding. That includes using correct terminology.

We are ready to discuss the amazing process which takes place when the body of a man and a woman respond to sexual arousal. Knowing how God created and planned, we would not expect this to be a haphazard set of responses with no rhyme, reason, or consistency. And in fact it is not random. Rather it is a predictable sequence of physical changes which take place when lovemaking is contemplated and carried out. But since God did not make carbon-copy sets of people, there is also some room for variability. I like that about God too.

For study convenience the human sexual response of both men and women has been divided into four phases. These are the excitement, plateau, orgasmic, and resolution phases. Two fundamental events will take place, physiologically. One will involve blood congestion in deep as well as superficial veins. The other will be the increase in muscle tension both of the voluntary and involuntary muscles. These changes would be expected with reference to healthy persons without negative feelings about the sexual process. To make comparison somewhat easier, we will look at each of these phases from both the male and female viewpoint and then go to the next one and treat it in the same manner. (This is from Masters and Johnson's explanatory description.)

I. Excitement Phase

The excitement phase is initated in response to certain

stimuli to the senses. Touching is a most important avenue of experiencing arousal. Some areas of the body have a richer supply of nerve endings, and greater arousal is possible. Other senses are to a lesser extent a means of stimulation. Vision, hearing, smell, and taste, while they do not operate reflexively, can call to mind experiences with which sexual arousal is associated. A shared love song, a single red rose, a walk on the beach, a freshly baked cinnamon roll, terms of endearment—all these can recall to memory a sexual experience or a feeling of tenderness and caring for the presenter which can begin to motivate a desire for sexual union.

Emotional arousal is sometimes not sufficiently understood. Physical stimulation is generally not sufficient for a satisfying sexual experience. Emotional states such as the feeling of being cherished, trusted, respected—these will enhance a relationship. Anxiety, hostility, feelings of self-devaluation can block off response patterns.

We tend to feel that men and women arouse to different types of stimuli. Since this feeling would seem to charge God with a bit of poor engineering, we might do well to take another look at it. Indeed, though the study in this area has not been exhaustive, recent findings indicate that differences are not physical so much as cultural and social expectations and experiences. Differences in response between the sexes does not seem to be greater than differences between people of the same sex. (See Katchadourian H. A., *Fundamentals of Human Sexuality*, p. 55.) As husbands and wives have been more able to talk about their feelings, they have discovered that they usually respond to sensitive and loving overtures in much the same way.

The first indication of arousal in a woman is lubrication of the vagina. This wetness or "sweating" of the vaginal wall can begin as soon as ten to thirty seconds after a physiological or psychological stimulus event. This in no way indicates that a woman is ready for intercourse but simply denotes that her body is responding to sexual stimulation. Many more changes will follow before full arousal has been attained. In this phase, there will be changes in the clitoris, that tiny organ just above the vaginal entrance (see diagram). Though there is no "normal" size for this tiny bundle of nerve endings, it is generally described as the size of a small pea. The shaft of the clitoris is enclosed in the flesh beyond the glans, or tip. This little organ, then, begins to swell in most women (though in some so slightly as to be unobservable). The amount of swelling is not related to later responsiveness, however. The labia minora also begins to undergo congestion. Changes also begin in the vagina and enlargement in the width and length of the vaginal barrel commences. The outer lips, or labia major, tend to "open up" in a receptive gesture.

Elsewhere on the woman's body changes also occur. Breast changes may take place during this phase. This could include nipple erection, increase in breast size and sensitivity. A general tensing of the muscles of the body, and an increase of pulse and breathing rate is usually present. Sometimes a "sex flush" which has a somewhat measleslike appearance appears on the upper part of the abdomen and breasts. Each of these initial changes heralds the way for later sexual intercourse.

Now let us consider the male response in this excitement phase. The very first sign is the erection of the penis. This involves an increase in the size of the penis as well as its change in angulation from the body. This also takes place within seconds after appropriate stimulus. A smaller penis may more than double its length, while one that may be longer in its limp state, will not undergo that much enlargement during erection. In other words, an erectile state is a great equalizer of penis size. The scrotum will become thickened and more tense so that there is a shortening and pulling up to the body of the entire scrotal sac. This scrotal sac contains the testes, and at times it is found that one of these testes will draw up farther and will be higher than the other one. There is no significance in this.

Stimulated males in this stage can also experience nipple errection. The flush we discussed earlier in reference to female arousal also may be observed. Again we find an increase in heart rate and mucular tension.

II. Plateau State

During this stage, many of the processes which began in the excitement stage are now carried through to their conclusion. It should be mentioned here that there is no distinct, specific moment when phase one becomes phase two. In fact, these two first stages are probably the least clearly defined of any. But while the point at which one phase enters the next is not clear-cut, the emphasis is on the concept that the plateau stage is the necessary time lapse which should exist before excitement phase goes into the orgasmic phase. The plateau stage should not be a quick pass through to the orgasmic stage. The touching and loving verbal interchange should not be a hurried, perfunctory experience. An impoverished repertoire of lovemaking sometimes lays the groundwork for boredom and dysfunction or failure.

In the female, then, breast changes will continue with further swelling of the areola surrounding the nipples. The sex flush will become even more pronounced. Muscular tension is sometimes experienced literally from head to toes. The heartbeat may be accelerated to 160 or 170 beats per minute, and the breathing may become heavier and more frequent.

The clitoris now seems to be retracted beneath the clitoral hood. This phenomenon takes place as the clitoris is elevating and drawing farther back from the vaginal entrance. It continues to respond to stimulation, at times from the pressure of the up and down movement of the clitorial hood during the thrusting of the penis in the vagina. The "orgasmic platform" is formed by the engorgement of the outer one third of the vagina, which can add as much as a total inch to the vaginal length.

Meanwhile, the uterus elevates, causing "tenting" of the inner two thirds of the vagina. This is a period of intensely pleasurable feelings. Aided by the knowledge that she is treasured and held dear by her husband, a woman is truly conscious that "I am my beloved's and my beloved is mine." She can, indeed feed "among the lilies." Song of Solomon 6:3.

Male changes during the plateau stage also include the same total-body muscular tension responses as we noted in the female. Heart rate increases, and breathing accelerates and intensifies. If the man's nipples did not become erect earlier, they may do so at this time. His testes may further elevate. In more prolonged lovemaking, the man may notice that the scrotal sac may relax several times during this time, and he may notice that the erection may become more flaccid and then return to a harder state. These are all natural phenomena.

Increased blood engorgement causes the corona of the penile gland to become more pronounced. A few drops of pre-orgasmic fluid may emerge from the male urethra and penis. This fluid may contain large numbers of active sperm. This is important to know if pregnancy is not desired at this time. This emission is involuntary, and the man may not be aware of its occurrence. Continued stimulation at this stage of sexual arousal will almost always lead to orgasm.

III. Orgasmic Phase

This third phase is at the culmination of complete sexual arousal. It is as though a goblet is being filled drop by drop to its very limit. When this limit is reached, overflow takes place. This consummate experience is reserved, in its fullest physical and emotional intensity, for humans. I like to think of it as a special gift for a thinking, emoting creation. God could have decided upon a joyless intercourse experience engaged in only for procreation. He did not. He could have settled upon another modality of impregnation which involved only a cursory contact. He did not. He designed that this act of one-fleshness bring two committed people together people in a throb of unity. And this union He designed to be the means of bonding a man and woman to one another in pleasure, in potentional, and in praise.

In the female, a momentary feeling of suspension is followed by rythmic, muscular contractions in the orgasmic platform. There may be from three to fifteen of these. After each contraction the interval lengthens and the intensity diminishes somewhat. Contractions also occur in the uterus and the entire perineal area. A feeling of warmth is sometimes felt starting in the pelvic area and spreading over the entire body.

In the male, the end of the plateau stage brings with it a feeling of inevitability—a point at which he realizes that ejaculation will take place imminently. Contractions begin which will drive the seminal fluid into the urethra with some force. The interval of these contractions is approximately the same as for the female, i.e. eight tenths of a second initially, and lengthing time between subsequent contractions. Perhaps it should be mentioned here that during sexual arousal, when the penis is errect, the urethra is no longer in service to pass urine. This is a seperate body process. This is assured by the closure of an inner sphincter muscle inhibiting urine passage.

Both men and women experience at this time a peak acceleration of heart rate and blood pressure, accompanied by rapid, deep breathing. Tightening muscles may cause the facial features to became taut. Hands of either partner may reach and grasp for the other as though to facilitate further this ultimate drawing together. One-fleshness has occurred.

IV. Resolution Phase

This last phase of sexual arousal finishes the sequence. In the female, the body now begins to return to the nonstimulated state. The sex flush disappears, breasts return to normal size, and muscular tension is released. The heartbeat, blood pressure, and respiration all quickly normalize. Some women find that a fine coat of perspiration appears on the body. The congestion which has been experienced in the genital area disappears within a few minutes. This means that the clitoris, the minor and major labia, and the vagina return to the pre-aroused state.

In the male, there is also reversal of tissue changes. There is a primary loss of erection, while the scrotal changes to the nonstimulated state are somewhat slower to occur. As in the female, the sex flush disappears and the muscular tension dissipates. Normal heart rate, blood pressure, and respiration return. A film of perspiratory moisture may also occur over the body.

Now, while the above presents a narrative of sexual arousal of man and woman, it is certainly not a model or a norm that a person must try to achieve in detail. It is simply a description of what usually happens.

I have tried in this chapter to restrict the discussion to physiological aspects of the sexual experience, although this is very difficult, since the physiological and the psychological are distinctly integrated. We have noted how carefully God planned and engineered body parts for the sexual pleasure of a husband and wife. That it is not always a joyous experience indicates that there is something amiss with how this design is understood and carried out.

How It Is for Women

"How can I know what pleases my wife? We don't seem to be able to talk about it." Many husbands are asking this question. And since I have had the opportunity to talk with wives about how they desire to experience their sexuality, I am going to share with you information that I think will be most helpful. Hopefully this will make three main contributions. (1) It will inform men in a way to help them better understand their wives. (2) It will help wives realize that they are not alone in what they are experiencing. And (3) equally important, I hope that it will help wives and husbands enter into dialogue with one another, for they are the best experts on their individual responses. Let me emphasize that last statement. We are all unique persons with our own reactions to stimuli. Some of the things in this chapter may not "fit" everyone exactly. That's where the dialogue is important.

Women repeatedly affirmed that the way they feel about their husbands sexually is related to the quality of their interpersonal relationship. Let's define that last phrase. A good interpersonal relationship would encompass concern, respect, feeling cherished and understood, with fairly good communication—at least most of the time! This would preclude being told "It's just stupid to say that you can't parallel park" or "What's the matter with you that you can't balance a check book?" A good relationship would not be congruent with being ignored, pushed aside, or told that you couldn't cook a decent meal or clean house the way mother used to do. To expect women to be eager for sexual activity after that kind of communication is unrealistic. Nor do women like sex to be seen as a wordless means of a husband 'saying, "I'm sorry." Dr. Richard Udry in *Social Context of Marriage* extrapolated from studies to reach some interesting conclusions. When there is a good interpersonal relationship between the married ones, certain things follow: The levels of sexual desire in both wife and husband are more congruent. There is increased orgasmic ability. And couples are more inclined to agreement on the amount of sexual activity and the ways of making love. What happens inside the bedroom cannot be separated from what happens outside the bedroom. When the hours of the day are gratifying, the sexual experience will more likely be joyous.

Further, women wish that intimacy could be enjoyed as a total experience, not merely as a physical one. There should be feelings of closeness and cooperation in other of life's aspects. Common experiences could include working together on some home project, being together by choosing similar recreational pursuits, intellectual enhancement through classes and reading, and certainly sharing and discussing spiritual concerns. The Clinebells in their book *The Intimate Marriage* point the way to a host of directions that a husband and wife can move in fostering a feeling of togetherness. Emotional intimacy which infers a closeness to the other in feelings is of great importance. To be able to share with your lover your inner dreams, joys, disappointments—each emotional feeling creates a closeness which cannot but enhance the sexual experience. One-fleshness can then have its truest expression.

A woman wishes to be treated as a total person rather than a set of genital organs. Since a man tends more generally to think of sexual pleasure as limited to the genital organs, he does not always understand why this is not acceptable for his wife. Female congestive response is more diffuse. She experiences erotic feelings in other body areas as well. In an initial love advance a woman prefers being held close, stroked, and patted while hearing loving words.

If the sexual progression should begin with a glance or a touch, we could think of the course of love play as being on a continuum. From that overture there may follow a light kiss, stroking of the neck and shoulders, more loving kisses. Caressing of the breasts and the lower torso should occur before sexual intercourse is even initiated. Some surveys indicate that a woman from the first stage of love play to complete arousal generally needs between twenty and forty minutes. One can see, then, that the energy spent on preparing the way for the climatic union can consume some time. Most women deeply appreciate this opportunity to enjoy fully this emotional and physical climate which affirms their femininity—their sexuality.

It is hard for women to understand why their husbands seem to be in such a hurry in lovemaking. If it is such a glorious experience, why rush it? Why not savor each passing moment for itself, not simply as a stage that one has to pass through to get to the "main event." Lovemaking is *all* the main event, from the first light touch to the quiet relaxation in one another's arms. A lovemaking experience—which includes alternating and repeated periods of stimulation, resting, verbal communication, "teasing," and intensity—is a memorable one. Each can tell the other how a touch, a stroke, a caress pleases. But a wife's response should not be compared by her husband with a textbook's or manual's description of the "ideal" sexual response. Many women have been deeply resentful of having been compared with another woman's response at this time.

This could be a former wife, another sexual liaison, or even a friend's reported description of *his* wife's sexual behavior. A woman does not wish her sexual experience to be a matter of discussion between her husband and his friends, either in jest or seriously. It seems tragic that sometimes people can discuss their sexual problems more freely with others than with one another.

Now let us talk of some specific physical aspects of the sexual act. The most sensitive area of the vagina is the outer third. Generally stimulation directed to that area is more arousing. The inner and outer lips of the vagina are also sensitive. The touch should be gentle and tender, rather than firm and hard. Many times to a man whose evaluation of a good meaningful handshake is one that grasps firmly and resolutely, a "gentle" touch means something not quite gentle enough. For this reason it is a good idea to enquire what "gentle" or tender means to each person. Try touching one another's hands in a tender manner. With feedback from his wife a well-meaning husband will be able to differentiate between being tender and too purposeful.

The same caution should be used in approaching stimulation of the clitoris. "Clitoris" is related to an ancient Greek word for "key"—and indeed it is the key for sexual feeling for women. It is most interesting to relize that this tiny organ is the only piece of tissue in the body of either a male or female which has for pleasurable feelings its one and only purpose. It receives and transmits these thrilling sensations if appropriately stimulated. Think what that means! In planning for a woman's part in the sexual experience, God made provision, through this organ, for her to be a full partner in ecstatic feelings. The full realization that God planned and created this amazing structure should long since have laid to rest the old myth that sex is for the man's need and enjoyment and that women must merely do her part to give him his pleasure. You recall that Paul is careful to say in 1 Corinthians 7:5, that *neither* husband nor wife was to defraud the other, that each should be aware of what God had planned for the other in this experience.

The clitoral versus the vaginal orgasm is also myth. There is only one orgasm, and that orgasm generally involves the whole vulvar area with pulsations being felt specifically in the orgasmic platforms of many women. Sometimes men, realizing the importance of this very sensitive little organ, concentrate on it too intensely. They may forget that the whole body feeling is important for women and that attention to other sensitive areas does not take away from the clitoral contribution but adds to it. Because of its extreme sensitivity, it is sometimes uncomfortable or even painful to put direct pressure on the clitoris, particularly without lubrication. You will recall that in the plateau phase the clitoris literally retracts under the clitoral hood, thus removing it somewhat from ready accessibility for direct contact. Indirect stroking, pressure on the mons area and the rhythmic pressure that occurs during penile thrusting is frequently sufficient to bring orgasm—particularly when ample time has been taken and loving attention paid to the earlier stages of lovemaking.

We must speak now of the orgasmic phenomenon. Orgasm has become a household word in the last decade. I am not sure that too much has not been made of it. It represents almost the Holy Grail search, an obsessive crusade to reach the highly touted orgasmic occurrence. To downplay the beauty of this transcending experience would be to defraud God's creation. But to overplay it, to invest it with unrealistic and exaggerated expectations, is to court disappointment and disillusionment.

A woman's capacity to be multi-orgasmic that is, to be stimulated to orgasm more than once before the resolution stage, has become a common theme in the literature. It has almost become a numbers game to reach orgasms after this manner. Some women who formerly felt satisfied with one respectable orgasm are beginning to feel that they are somehow less feminine, less sexual, if they cannot approximate someone else's feat. It is common to hear such words as "achieve," "attain," "reach," when speaking of orgasms as though they were the whole emphasis in lovemaking.

This saddens me. I do not like to think of sexual experience as being in the competitive realm. An occasion of lovemaking should be an experience in feelings—physical, emotional, and spiritual. Sandra McDermott in *Female Sexuality* (New York: Simon & Schuster, 1970) reports on a study done in England where over two hundred women were interviewed. Most of these said that they were as sexually satisfied, or fulfilled, with one orgasm as with several. What is generally more important to women than the number of orgasms is the circumstances preceding this phase. It is the warmth, loving, and holding that accompanies the love play—not the orgasm in itself—which makes the whole experience so satisfying.

Some men think that their lovemaking ability undergoes enhancement if they can feel that they have stimulated their wives into more than one orgasm during the lovemaking period. In most cases the woman would like to play an equal part in choosing that option or choosing simply to bask in the contentment she already feels.

It has been helpful for men to realize that women generally have more variability in their experience of orgasm than men do. I like to think of the response of orgasm as being on a continuum. On one end of the continuun is the quiet, gentle relaxation and on the other end a great marvelous explosion. The orgasm can vary in the experience of each woman at different times, or from woman to woman.

Men tend to feel that they have been more successful if their wives respond with more movement, sound, or general displays of emotion. But response does not always equal feeling.

Some women have trained themselves to be passive and more subdued. Some are more inhibited by nature. From my duty in delivery rooms I can remember that some women screamed and cried during childbirth while others quietly awaited the event. Neither reacted wrongly.

I have sometimes used the following illustration with husbands who are not sure that their wives are enjoying lovemaking: Suppose you are sitting behind two box seats at a World Series baseball game. In each of these seats a woman intently watches every movement in the game. The time is crucial; it is a tie game with two outs, and the man at bat carries the series in his hands. After a full count—three balls and two strikes—the batter connects with the pitch and sails that ball over the bleachers. Now, assuming that their team was the winner, watch these two women. One jumps up and down, screams, hugs her escort in jubilation, and continues to cheer loudly. The other smiles and claps her hands. Do you *know* which has the greatest satisfaction from that home run? No, you can only speculate. Each enjoyed the event in her own way. Response is more a personal variation than an indication of enjoyment. Women should not be pressured to feel that they must respond in a way that fits someone's expectations. Also there will be times when, because of worry, preoccupation, or weariness, orgasms do not provide the same amount of intensity as previously. The sexual experience can still be beautiful. Husbands should not be concerned if this happens occasionally.

In former years many thought that unless lovers could experience their orgasms at the same moment, their lovemaking was impaired or even somewhat neurotic. Fortunately, simultaneous orgasms are no longer considered that hallmark of mature sexuality. When one takes into account the difference in the cultural background, social preparedness, and individual readiness of the two partners involved in each sexual occasion, it is difficult to see how these two persons could come to climax at identical times, on demand. Since orgasm is such a personal experience, many partners feel that their enjoyment is doubled by tending to their own pleasure in a separate moment and then being aware of their spouse's rapture. I believe that this is what one-fleshness implies—joy in one's lover equal to joy in one's self. Sometimes women who are nonorgasmic try to reassure their husbands that the sexual union they share is yet full of delightsome pleasure for them. For some men, this is difficult to accept. They somehow feel that if they could just be better lovers, their wives would be more fulfilled. While each is responsible to do what she or he can to enhance the other's pleasure, neither is totally responsible for the other's orgasm. So many factors are involved, some which may have played a vital role long before these two married. After carefully attending to all the factors over which they have control, let them, then, accept the wife's declaration of satisfaction and continue to make each sexual experience an occasion of joy and celebration.

Once the orgasm phase has been consummated, the sexual experience is still not completed. Often women express a wish that their husbands would make more of the time immediately following orgasm. Women usually subside from their aroused state more slowly than men, particularly emotionally. They can experience prolonged and profound pleasure in relaxing in their husband's arms. Men seem at times not as sensitive to this need as they might be. When men omit this afterglow time, women can interpret this as switching off the emotional component of love and thus reducing lovemaking to a mechanical experience.

What an ideal time for gentle stroking, tender holding, and loving declarations! What an opportune interval for the partners to discuss their love and the profound experience that it has just brought them. What a precious moment to breath a prayer of thankfulness for the gift of sexuality.

There are several additional important areas that I must also mention in womens' behalf. Women in general realize that they are usually slower to consider innovative ways of vitalizing a lovemaking routine. This may mean a different time of day, a new setting, or an addition to their lovemaking repertoire. I believe this to be a spin-off of the responsibility women have always carried for "holding the line." Many women reading this will recall that their mothers told them that they were responsible if "things went too far." Having through many years been the "watch dogs of morality," women have been conditioned to proceed very carefully in approval of ideas new to them. When presented with a new proposal, they have generally put the suggestion—or demand—through several evaluations: "Is it decent?" "Is it pure?" "Is it holy?" Answers to these questions do not usually come quickly or easily. Nothing worthwhile is gained by argument, teasing, nagging, or threatening. When a woman feels that she can trust her lover to cherish her, to want the best for her and to respect her, she will be more likely to acquiesce and even to become—if slowly—enthusiastic about love-making creativity.

Women also wish that their husbands would realize that a refusal of the sexual offer does not mean the total rejection of the husband as a sexual partner or a worthwhile person. Sometimes to postpone lovemaking is another way of saying, "I have too high a regard for this celebration of love to enter into it when I am tired, preoccupied, or ill." At times like this a woman may wish to snuggle and lie close to her husband in lieu of entering into sexual congress.

This leads us to an important point. If I hear one single plea more than any other from wives, it is this: Can't there be some loving communication between wives and husbands that is not always directed at intercourse? In other words, does sexuality always have to lead to sex? Listen to these comments I have heard from wives: "I wish that there could be some loving without it being an inevitable prelude of falling into bed!" "I feel like a sex machine—you put in a kiss and get out a sexual event!" "I long to be loved simply because I am considered a lovable person, not always a bed partner!"

Well, men, there you have it! I have had women tell me that they sometimes reject or respond coldly to a certain kind of a hug or kiss because they know what is expected. "Pecks on the cheek are harmless," one said, "but watch out for that one on the back of the neck!" Other women have said that they have to be careful in their evidencing tender and loving demonstrations at those times when they are not ready to follow through with them. How sad! What a loss of love nourishment—the pomegranates and grapes of the love fruit that Solomon and his bride extolled. Couples need—yes, need—to be often engaged in hugging, patting, kissing, stroking, and "sporting" with one another. Clues will soon evolve—if words are too difficult—as to whether one of the "lovingnesses" will culminate this event or whether they are both aroused to continue intensifying the expressions of their love.

In his exhortation to married folk, Peter tells husbands, in 1 Peter 3:7, "Likewise, ye husbands, dwell with them [wives] according to knowledge." This most certainly should include a knowledge of the wife's sexual responses if this important part of their interaction is to be joyous.

And How It Is for Men

"It seems to me that men are stuck with the label of sexual villains!" These words were spoken to me by a troubled young man who had heard, once too often, what unfeeling, demanding brutes men are. It is true that while a number of things I have said about men are applicable to some, they should certainly not be applied to all.

I believe that our culture also asks some unreasonable things of men. They are supposed to know all about sexuality and to lead in the sexual experience when married. And yet no one knowledgeable has supplied them with all the necessary data. It is assumed they will know what their wives appreciate in lovemaking without being told by them. They must be strong, unemotional, and never admit hurt in the everyday world. And yet they must know how to be loving and tender in intimate moments. If a man's wife has a problem in finding sexual fulfillment—that's his fault. And if *he* has sexual problems—that's also his fault. He tends to feel he is not "half a man." You see, under such circumstances he can't win.

Only recently has the literature taken a second look and tried to find out how men presently feel. A preponderance of men perceive themselves to be very interested in their wives' enjoyment. They report that they also enjoy being caressed and are not interested in speeding through sexual intercourse.

One survey found that men feel guilty, selfish, empty, and inferior when they feel that they are not good lovers (*Redbook* magazine, February/March 1978). Men, in the generic sense, should not really be characterized as selfish and insensitive in lovemaking. Of course many never were; but, unfortunately, some still are.

Let us look at some of the suggestions men have offered which they feel would enhance their enjoyment of sexuality. Men would like the myth dispelled that men are always ready, willing, and able to have sex. This myth implies that men don't want to enjoy lovemaking in its fuller aspects. It also fosters the notion that they don't want to be encouraged about their ability. These notions simply are not so. Frequently it is because men feel restricted and rationed that they sometimes seem to be pushing sexual activity at every opportunity. When they are secure in their feelings of manliness and often receive a warm and loving reception, their advances don't need to be so insistent or frenetic.

Men realize that they have been accused of rushing through loveplay with insufficient attention given to holding and to loving verbalizations. But their locker-room education ingrained in them the feeling that "fast" was seen as more manly than "slow." How many fathers reading these words have taken the time to explain to their sons the loving, unhurried accompaniment to intercourse that wives appreciate? How many learned this from their fathers?

Men have expressed the feeling that they receive "hurry and get it over with" messages from their wives and that for this reason they don't prolong the activity. Wives will have to review what in their attitudes may be contributing to this complaint. Where husbands are beginning to pay more heed to wives' love-play needs, wives should be quick to reinforce this fresh approach with appreciative remarks and praise for this thoughtfulness. People usually repeat what is applauded.

Men too are discovering that their entire bodies enjoy stroking and touching. They would appreciate finding out even more about how pleasant it is for their own faces, necks, shoulders, etc., to be gently caressed. Sometimes they say it is a little embarrassing to ask for this kind of touching. How much more would they appreciate such initiative coming from their wives.

Some husbands feel that since children have come into the home, sexual loving has become secondary. Often, they tell me, when they suggest lovemaking or even while in its process, they are met with such remarks as these: "The baby is fussing." "They're awake!" "They might hear us." "I've really got to talk to you about Johnny's temper tantrums."

If lovemaking is relegated to second place when children come, its beauty may never again be recaptured, even after the children are long gone. Both mother and father can take the responsibility to plan uninterrupted times together. Both need to take a cooperative interest in one another's suggestions until a good plan is worked out.

There is true feminine beauty in the loving response of a wife to her husband. This does not include retreating, pushing away, giggling, or grunting "nuh-uh." Such responses can make a man wonder why he stays faithful. A verbal response such as "Well, OK, if you really want to," or "Not again!" make him feel something less than ten feet tall. Of course a wife does have the right to postpone lovemaking under adverse circumstances. But she also has the loving responsibility to do so in a way that does not suggest rejection.

Let's try some alternative responses to see if they might sound more positive:

"You seem to have lots of energy today; I wish I did. I'm exhausted after canning [ironing, cleaning, or whatever]; can I take a raincheck, sweetheart?"

"I don't feel like lovemaking tonight, John; but I certainly feel like snuggling and telling you how much I love you."

"You've got a great idea; it's just not the right time for me tonight. How about waking up early tomorrow morning? I'll set the alarm!"

"I'm so glad you want to make love with me. It makes me feel very special, but—"

And then how about the *wife* planning a love tryst. "Don't be late tonight! The children are eating with grandma, and I'm planning a candlelight dinner for us. We won't pick up the children until bedtime."

Wife, watch the joy in his eyes, and connect with the happy anticipation you can enjoy as you carry out your plan. It has the ring of Solomon 7:12, don't you think? "Let us get up early to the vineyards; let us see if the vine flourish, whether the tender grape appear, and the pomegranates bud forth: there will I give thee my loves."

Even when wives may be willing to engage in a love-in, husbands sometimes feel that their wives' passivity sends out messages of disinterest. This impression may carry residuals of the feeling that to be active and involved is not quite "ladylike." All of this can be modified if the wife is willing to be open and responsive to her husband's needs. She can learn to give more evidence of her interest and pleasure. She can discover ways to express her joyousness, even though her personality style may be more reserved. Incidentally, this communicating should be done in a manner consistent with her personality type, but she *can* discover ways to express her joyousness. She too will be glad to hear how her husband appreciates her efforts in being more active and communicative.

From initially participating with general statements of love and pleasure, a wife can advance to more specific requests regarding what pleases her in lovemaking. One woman told me, "Well, he should know what I want!" This implies that her husband is either instinctively all-knowing or a mind reader, and few persons can measure up to these amazing qualifications. A husband or wife can only *know* what experience has taught them through observing or listening to their spouse's feedback. Our limited knowledge in the area of sexuality, as well as our reticence, does make communication difficult. One of my hopes for this book is that it will help to make talking easier.

Another way for a wife to promote a knowledge of response is to guide her husband's hands with her own, demonstrating to him the pressure, the movements, and the area which can best enhance her good feelings.

Wives have told me that their attempts to get a message like this across to their husbands sometimes seem to cause an incensed or resentful reaction of being "told what to do." This is no doubt a response to ingrained male feelings of responsibility for being "in charge" and for being expected to have all of the answers. It might also result from the way her message is given. "Not that way!" or "You're stroking me all wrong!" tends to make a husband feel more scolded than guided. Both husbands and wives need to be aware of the strong impact of tone, inflection, and manner. A gesture of impatience or a strained, harsh word communicates displeasure and antagonism.

Read the Song of Solomon and note how many human senses the author appeals to in his description of lovemaking. One does not get the impression that the interaction of this bride and groom was lackluster, monotonous, or stodgy. Solomon communicates vitality, activity, and awareness. These lovers were *involved* with one another. In the last chapter we spoke of the difficulty wives sometimes undergo in being enthusiastic about creativity and variation in lovemaking. Some husbands do feel that their wives are more interested in creative menu-making and flower arranging than in creative lovemaking. Let's explore that.

There are only a limited number of ways that a lovemaking routine can be varied. You can change the place, the time, the setting, and the techniques. Many couples have reported that a vacation can add interest to their sexual repertoire. But one does not need to leave home (though several weekends a year away from home together, and alone together, are highly recommended). Even in one's own home plans can be made to change the setting to another room—to a secluded garden spot at midnight or before a glowing fireplace. Some men feel that the only time their lovemaking is welcome is at night. Others go so far to suggest that their wives are willing at night only because it is dark then. But a brand-new morning can be hailed by lovemaking. A planned afternoon is equally pleasant with the sun streaming in the window. And nighttime can be varied with candles, music, incense, and a full moon glowing in a stream of soft light through the window.

Somewhere we have accepted as almost sacrosanct the idea that lovemaking should take place in the male-superior position, and we sometimes add "without hands." Some call this the "missionary position"—the one which the missionaries taught indigenous peoples when it seemed that they were having too much fun with their "variations." It is as though fun and enjoyment are not compatible with devout lovemaking. Others have suggested that since man has felt himself to be superior and in authority over woman, this way of making love more truly reflects what is right and proper. I cannot accept this interpretation. Too many men have suggested that they would be pleased with this "role-reversal" in love play. Making love while the two are lying on their side (either front-to-front or back-to-front, spoon fashion), while facing one another sitting on a low chair, or with the wife lying across the bed with her buttocks even with the side of the bed and her husband approaching her in a kneeling position—all of these and other variations can be developed and tried to vary the love feast.

In the matter of caressing one another, some wives show reluctance to touch their husband's body, particularly around the genital area. It is as though some magical line around the middle of the body above which touching is decent and "pure," but below which is somewhat evil or depraved. God formed these parts of the body—yes, even the genitals—with His own hands. When two people are one flesh, do they not have the privilege, the joy, of responding to this one-fleshness with wonder and delight?

Sometimes caressing one another's genitals is being confused with masturbation. Let us quickly dispel this myth. The term "mutual masturbation" has sometimes been thus interpreted. There is no such thing as mutual masturbation in lovemaking when two people are involved with one another. Masturbation is, by definition, a process of self-stimulation. It is autoerotic. Tenderly and affectionately giving one another pleasure, either by turn or simultaneously through manual touching, is a beautiful way to express love for and delight in one another.

I cannot leave the area of lovemaking techniques without mentioning oral caressing. I am asked about it frequently. A survey done by Nancy Van Pelt indicated that around 50 percent of Seventh-day Adventists employ this as a means of enhancing their love-play. (See *The Journal of the Association of Adventist Behavioral Scientists*, June 1978, p. 25). I believe that this is an area in which no one should make pronouncements for another. Where we have no biblical instruction or other definitive counsel, I believe that we should be careful in setting guidelines which suit our own biases. For some couples kissing and caressing with their lips the entire body of their beloved can be a joyous experience—this part of their love play expresses for them an all encompassing love. For others, or for one or the other of the couple, it is possible that they cannot overcome feelings of being repelled by the genital area, or at least oral contact with it. I believe that this decision should be honored by either spouse.

I would be concerned if one party was trying to force this type of loveplay on an unwilling partner. Sometimes it becomes almost an obsession for one partner or the other to initiate this variation. I believe that preoccupation with this demand—or any other—is saying something negative about the whole relationship, not simply about the sexual aspect of the relationship. Each spouse should respect a decision made with equanimity and in good grace and should happily continue lovemaking in ways which each can accept joyously.

Once in a while a husband expresses the wish that his wife weren't so disapproving of her own body. Such a husband feels that his wife is too critical of her own breasts, hips, general body proportions or whatever, to the point where their sexual relationship is affected. Few men, very few, are looking for a perfect set of measurements. They are rarely appraising her negatively—mostly they appreciate loving, caring, and joyousness in their sexual experiences with their wives. Sometimes men wonder if this self-critical attitude is the reason their wives insist on wearing flannel nightgowns or coverall pajamas! They appreciate their wives' beauty unadorned and would like to have the opportunity to do so more often. They are desirous of enjoying parts of their own one-fleshness—their wives' part. It is hard for them to understand the reluctance they frequently meet even after years of marriage. As do women, men enjoy cleanliness, fragrance, and attractive nightwear. And most men are pleased to have their cleanliness, fragrance, and just-shaved smoothness appreciatively mentioned by their wives.

I think it is important for wives to know that men, too, have concerns about their sexuality and need feelings of approval. Sometimes, due to fatigue, anxiety, or illness, a man may find himself unable to complete a sexual experience. It may be almost impossible for most women even to begin to realize what this means to a man. A man's self-concept is directly connected to his sexual ability. That is not the way it should be—but it is.

A man's measure should be evaluated by his caringness, his compassion, his responsiblity, and his integrity. A man can have all of the above and still feel a failure if he cannot measure up to his ideal of "masculinity" in the sexual arena—and I use the last word carefully. Many times a man feels himself in a competitive struggle to measure up to his expectations, to the anticipation that he believes his wife has, and to the cultural norms that have been thrust upon him. What an impossible load! More understanding on the part of wives when the sex act is interrupted by an inability to continue or a premature ejaculation takes place would lighten much self-recrimination on the part of husbands. Knowing that it happens to every male at times is something that both husband and wife should be aware of. We are not here talking about chronic dysfunction but the occasional difficulty.

Occasional worry about the adequate size of his penis is not abnormal for a husband. But her husband's penis size is not something a woman generally worries about, and she finds it hard to understand why this may be significant to him. When both spouses realize that the most sensitive area of the vagina is the outer one third, they can both get a better perspective. Again, reassurance of her appreciation of his masculinity and his concern for her sexual fulfillment are welcome indeed.

I am always filled with awe when I study God's plan for two people to unite in sexual love. A secretary once misunderstood my dictation to be saying, "I am always filled with 'ahs.' " Well, that too! Ah, yes, the wonderful way of a man and a maid!

Systems Gone Wrong

One out of every two—the figures aren't heartening. But Masters and Johnson estimate that one out of every two married couples in the United States is sexually unfulfilled. Something is unsatisfactory about the way the partners are relating to one another sexually. Chronic sexual difficulties are to be blamed. Some of these conditions may simply be troublesome; others may interfere critically. In some cases the disorder may have been evident immediately upon marriage. In others it may be a symptomatology which has developed in the course of the wedded life.

Sometimes we will hear either a wife or husband say, "Well, its his problem." Or, "There's nothing wrong with me. Help her." I do not believe that there can be a sexual problem that does not deeply affect both partners. Anxiety, guilt, blame, hurt, disappointment, concern are the emotions usually involved, and they will influence both spouses. Restoration to good functioning also involves a cooperative process.

Whenever there is a realization that sexual functioning is not satisfactory, the couple should make a prompt effort to discover whether the problem can be medically alleviated. Approximately 5 percent of sexual problems can be traced directly to physiological malfunction. How sad that either party in the marriage should continue to suffer dysfunction when the condition could be treated. It is sometimes difficult to discuss with a physician a problem involving such intimate information. But most physicians are now trained to be sensitive to patients who are trying to describe a symptomatology having to do with their sexuality and will try to make a patient feel less ill at ease.

We will divide the large area of sexual dysfunction into male and female dysfunction. My purpose is to give information about the problem areas so that readers can understand what can go wrong. Sometimes understanding can be effective in itself. But other times professional help may be needed.

Problems Women Experience in Sexual Functioning

I. Painful Intercourse

Painful intercourse, or dyspareunia, frequently has as its basis anxiety, tension, or fear. Physical conditions, however, can play a part. These can involve the vagina, uterus, or bladder. Some of these are irritation or infection of any parts of the vulva and the perineum; allergic sensitivity to methods of contraception, douching solution, or female deodorant preparations; too frequent douching (which can change the vaginal flora and encourage secondary infections); an intact hymen or sensitive remnants of the hymenal ring; lack of lubrication; senile changes in the vagina causing fragility and thinness; lesions or scar tissues in the vaginal opening; and polyps, cysts, tumors, or ulcerations of any part of the genital area or reproductive tract.

As soon as a woman experiences dyspareunia, she should immediately put herself in the care of a physician. The medical conditions can be treated for relief of pain in most cases. But the damage that is done to the emotional system when there is a constant repetition of the pain is harder to treat. When physical distress is repeatedly associated with the sexual experience, a woman begins to dread, dislike, resent, and withdraw. There are, unfortunately, no ready procedures or pills for these emotions.

II. Vaginismus

Vaginismus is the name given to another painful condition. It is an *involuntary* spasm of the vaginal muscles which causes closure of the vagina. I hope you noted the word *involuntary* in the last sentence. It is not a plight that a woman brings about consciously, even though a bewildered and discouraged husband sometimes accuses her of this. This condition can be even more confusing when, after the spasm disappears, some women are then able to engage in intercourse with comfort and gratification.

This problem can spring from an original physical complaint which conditions the vagina to respond with spasms—as though to protect itself from painful entry. Following alleviation of the original complaint, the conditioned response may continue even in the absence of pain. But conscious and unconscious factors may also create this troublesome reaction. If a woman perceives sex as a nasty, disgusting ordeal, if her religious and moral training has ingrained in her the idea that the sexual act is fraught with shame and impropriety, or if she has been exposed to the theory that "all men are brutes" and "all they want from you is sex," then she may find herself afflicted with vaginismus. Sometimes a traumatic experience during a physical examination under insensitive circumstances can carry some responsibility for this condition. Women who come for treatment sometimes give histories of traumatic molestation or rape.

Some women actually believe that they are physically "too small inside" for penile entry. They do not realize the wonderful adaptations of the human body which in almost all cases ensure compatibility between a healthy male and female.

When a marital relationship has built up resentment and hostility on the interpersonal level, the repressed tensions and deteriorating relationship can be an unconscious factor in impelling this spasmic response.

Again, it will be necessary to consult a physician, preferably one skilled in working with the emotional problems which may lie behind this condition. Sometimes doctors work as a team with counselors skilled in this area of interpersonal relationships. A thorough explanation of the female human sexual response pattern will help the woman to understand her physical adequacy. The physician will sometimes suggest a set of dilation tubes of increasing diameters. When the woman discovers that her vagina is able to comfortably accept increasingly larger dilators, she is usually convinced of the adequacy of her true capacity.

The husband should be closely involved in both the physical and emotional aspects of the treatment. His feelings are also important. He may have suffered a sense of inadequacy for not being able to prepare his wife sufficiently for intercourse. When both can be helped to understand the condition and to respond to one another with sensitivity and caring, the outlook can be very promising.

III. Preorgasmia and Nonorgasmia

Preorgasmia and nonorgasmia have replaced the term *frigidity*, which has judgmental and pejorative implications. Many women have had the frigidity label hurled at them because they decline sexual overtures for very defensible reasons. In other instances, a husband who would like to enjoy daily intercourse terms his wife frigid because her level of sexual desire is not as high as his. We are hearing currently of young unmarried ladies who have been accused of frigidity because they do not wish to engage in sex before marriage. You can see, then, that the word can hardly be used appropriately at this time.

I prefer the term *preorgasmia*, which has optimistic implications. It infers that to this point in time the woman may not have had the experience of orgasm, but the potential is there. This potentiality is precisely the case. Women are naturally capable of being orgasmic unless there is a physical impediment. And generally women *want* to experience their full potential as sexual persons. When a woman is indifferent, reluctant, or repulsed, conscious or unconscious influences are at work. Something in her background before her marriage or some negative experience in marriage has "taught" her to withhold her natural desire.

The group represented by the term "nonorgasmia" can be divided into (1) those who have not been able to experience orgasm (primary orgasmic dysfunction) and (2) those who have previously experienced orgasm but no longer do (secondary orgasmic dysfunction). There is one further classification that Masters and Johnson call "situational orgasmic dysfunction." Women in this condition only experience orgasm on "festival occasions"—vacations, anniversaries, or very specially staged happenings.

A whole gamut of predispositions to this problem exists among women. Some relate to physical discomfort and disease. Drugs and alcohol certainly can be responsible. But by far most underlying causes are not physical in nature. The following factors are sometimes linked with orgasmic dysfunction: (1) excessive fear of intercourse or pregnancy; (2) culturally inspired negative sexual messages from home or other environments or incorrectly interpreted religious proscriptions; (3) a poor self-image; (4) a very negative first sexual experience; (5) disappointment with mate (i.e., a woman's husband may not be as successful, as caring, or as sexually capable as she had imagined); (6) a great deal of masturbation with accompanying orgasms and subsequent dependance on one's own ability to achieve ideal stimulation. (7) ignorance of the body processes involved in sexual arousal and intercourse. We must not neglect to mention here that failure to allow sufficient time for sexual arousal can defraud a woman of fulfillment as can clumsiness, roughness, crudeness, vulgarity, or lack of loving emotional involvement on her husband's part.

A mother can sometimes program her daughter to lack of response by talking of her own sexual problems and suggesting that the daughter will probably experience the same condition. Parental influences can also include the father. A five-year study involving interviews of 300 women found that a woman was more apt to be consistently orgasmic when she had been "more likely than others to have been reared by fathers who were dependable, caring, demanding men who were insistent that their daughters meet certain moral standards and expectations." (See Seymore Fisher, *The Female Orgasm*, New York, Basic Books, 1973). These fathers were contrasted with those who were "unavailable for substantial relationships" and were seen as more "casual"—which attitude the daughters interpreted as disinvolvement and undependability. Coming from this background, they found learning to trust a sex partner more difficult than did the average woman. And as we have seen, lack of trust can devastate a marital relationship.

What can a woman do after medical consultation assures her that she is physically capable? A therapeutic approach would include a very careful assessment of factors in the past which, unknown to her, may be contributing to her situation, along with a thorough evaluation of her present knowledge of her own sexuality and a further exploration of her present attitudes. Her husband—who, we hope, is understanding and caring—would be expected to join her in the above areas of investigation. His insights would play a very important part in this process of therapy.

Both must realize that the goal is not so much orgasm as experiencing love and pleasure in one another. In fact, in a professional treatment situation, intercourse would be prohibited for a length of time until the couple had learned to appreciate other aspects of lovemaking.

This experience is called "sensate focus" by Masters and Johnson *(Human Sexual Response)* and "body caress" by Dr. William Hartman and Marilyn Fithian *(Treatment of Sexual Dysfunction)*. It is also known as a "non-demand pleasuring," in that there is no imposition to "produce" an orgasm. The couple is simply encouraged to relax and enjoy the good body feelings which come through gentle touching, stroking and caressing of the nongenital body parts.

It might be helpful here to describe this exercise, since it is not only therapeutic for a nonorgasmic situation, but helpful and pleasurable for couples who have no problem in that area.

In this exercise, the receiving partner lies on the bed in the prone (face downward) and then in the supine (face upward) position. In each of these positions, the giving partner kneels over the receiver and slowly and gently strokes the entire body from head to toe, avoiding the sexually sensitive areas. This is not to be confused with massage, which is firm and is directed purposefully at certain muscles. The pleasuring concept is based on the idea that people rarely realize what good body feelings can be experienced through the loving touch of a spouse and are too goal-directed to orgasm, making that their main emphasis. The fingers can caress sometimes in a circular pattern, sometimes in a long-stroking motion, or the giver could delicately apply a kneading movement. For the receiver this is not to be a passive, noninvolved experience. He or she should be intensely aware of the pleasure messages. The giving partner should consider the feelings being received through the senses of touch and sight. Among them are the realization of various skin textures and tones, the silky feeling of hair, the diversity of softness, firmness, and muscularity. This type of exercise should last at least half an hour for each person to receive pleasure.

After some days confined to this experience, the genital area would be included, but only included. It should not usurp the general body caressing. After several experiences of the exercise with this inclusion, the couple is frequently ready to proceed to intercourse. Because the body has been given a preparation of awareness to sexual stimulation, orgasm follows naturally.

I would like to emphasize that without attending to the interpersonal relationship between the husband and wife, the exercise has no magic quality. Both must be lovingly involved without blaming, recrimination, or feelings of martyrdom or hostility. No "Oh, what I go through for you," "How long is this going to take?" attitude must be permitted. Paramount must be this attitude in relationship: "I am as eager for your part of our one-fleshness to be fulfilled as I am for my own."

While many insightful and dedicated couples might be able to work out a problem in sexual dysfunction by themselves, many others will need professional help. If there is a long-standing problem with their relating to one another on the emotional level, they will need to work this out with a marriage counselor or a minister qualified in this kind of counseling.

Problems Men Experience in Sexual Functioning

When men experience sexual problems, they are for physical reasons in an even more vulnerable situation than women. Except in the rare cases of physical impedimenta, a woman is able to take part in sexual intercourse, even without being orgasmic. She can fill her wifely role, her feminine part. While under these circumstances her own enjoyment will depend upon her attitude and upon her husband's role in fulfilling her sexual needs—exclusive of orgasm—she is not deprived of the feeling of being a consenting, acting, and even eager partner. Hopefully she and her husband will continue to seek ways to enhance their lovemaking even if they do not elect to seek professional assistance. Sometimes after several years of marriage a woman's emotional acceptance of joyous sexuality can change from a preorgasmic status to one of full enjoyment.

The problems that a man encounters in his sexual functioning may often preclude his being able to express his masculinity through sexual intercourse. We have already mentioned the devastating effect this can have on his self-concept. He seems to judge the worthwhileness of his personhood—as defined by his ability to be a fully active sexual partner—in a more limited way than does a woman. Depression is more common in a nonfunctioning man than in a nonorgasmic woman.

To see how this could be so, recall how important society has, in the past, considered the parenting of children to be—a nonorgasmic woman can have a child, but an impotent man cannot sire one. Remember, too, that in the past women were thought to be incapable of enjoying sexual expression. Since remanants of this philosophy still haunt the thinking of some, perhaps many women, the inability to be orgasmic doesn't seem to be quite as crucial a matter for their feminine self-image as potency is for the masculine self-image.

The occasional incident of premature ejaculation and loss of erectile ability which we briefly mentioned in the last chapter can become chronic when anxiety takes over. After only one disappointing episode of lovemaking, a man may begin to worry about what might happen next time. This anxiety can affect his next erection sufficiently to cause his concern to be reinforced. And so further problems ensue. Worried attempts to prove his ability, due to the pressure that he exerts on himself, only exacerbate the problem. He may now begin self-recrimination, avoidance of and withdrawl from sexual contact.

His wife can be helpful at the beginning of this progression of symptoms by reminding him that all men go through occasional episodes of this type. She can reassure him verbally and through her active part in their lovemaking. But she also has the power to *add* to his anxiety by statements such as, "Well, you're getting older you know," or, "I hope that you do better than last." Or even in well-intentioned misguided concern she may flutter over him, reminding him repeatedly to see the doctor and wondering out loud if there is anything to the idea that artichokes have an aphrodisiac effect. (They don't! No foods have been demonstrated to enhance lovemaking ability, although a generally nutritious diet, which promotes good health, can indirectly enhance virility.)

I. Painful Intercourse

Although less frequently reported than female dyspareunia, painful intercourse, for men, should be mentioned here. Among the conditions which could be responsible are these: (1) an unretracted foreskin in an uncircumcised male (although uncircumcision in itself is not a problem), (2) irritation of the glans due to chemical contraceptives or an allergic reaction to soap or other toiletries, (3) lack of proper hygiene, leading to irritation or infection in an uncircumcised male, or (4) an injury resulting in bruising or muscle fracture of the penis. Several diseases also result in conditions which can result in painful intercourse for the husband. For this reason a physician should examine the first manifestation of unusual discomfort to determine its cause.

II. Ejaculatory Problems

A. Premature Ejaculation: This most common of male problems is difficult to define precisely. Prematurity may mean different things to different couples. While one couple could be quite satisfied with the length of time from intromission of the penis to ejaculation, another couple would feel that it happened much too quickly and thereby experience displeasure. There is a wide variety of delineations to go with the term. Some definitions time to the nearest second from the penile insertion to climax. Others use as their standard the number of penile thrusts before ejaculation. Perhaps the one which can be most easily personalized is Master's and Johnson's statement which designates ejaculation as premature if the husband cannot delay it long enough after penetration to please his wife at least half of the time.

None of these terms seems completely satisfactory. They do show us, however, that different people perceive this problem differently and that their expectations vary accordingly. Again we will reiterate that the *anxiety* which accompanies this condition, even when it occurs only occasionally, can nudge a couple's sex life into a cycle of failure.

A physical basis seldom exists for prematurity. Rare incidents of sensitivity due to chemical irritation or infection have been reported. Dr. Helen Kaplan hypothesized that a man with this problem has not learned to identify the sensations immediately preceding orgasm and for this reason has not learned ejaculatory control. (See Helen Kaplan, *The New Sex Therapy* [New York: Quadrangle, 1974].)

Some theorists have hypothesized that some teenage petting may actually condition prematurity. With sexual arousal, with body motion and pressure against the penis, a youth may have conditioned his ejaculation to rubbing and pressure rather than through penetration and containment. Since many of these clandestine incidents are hurry-up affairs with little thought for sustained pleasuring, this pattern of prematurity may become long-term and cause prematurity even in the marriage bed.

Other inciting factors have been suggested. One of these is a repeated practice of intensive and competive (timewise) masturbation. Infrequent intercourse has also been charged with encouraging prematurity. If intercourse is not engaged in with some regularity, a husband may become less sensitive to the approaching inevitability signals and lose a sense of control. In other cases, the buildup of sexual arousal due to infrequency can cause control to be too difficult.

Fortunately, of all male sexual dysfunctions, this responds best to treatment. Since the problem is both by husband and wife, the best chance for successful resolution lies with a loving and willing cooperation. A counselor may enhance and help the couple with a knowledge not only of the physical aspects of the problem but the emotional overlay as well. The wife needs to be helped to understand her important part, especially in avoiding the ways in which she might sabotage the therapeutic processes. She may be unaware of these. Her optimism, her encouragement, and her attitude during treatment are crucial.

The treatment designed by Masters and Johnson is known as the squeeze technique. The wife stimulates her husband's penis manually to the point of impending orgasm. At his signal she firmly grasps the glans of the penis between her thumb just above the coronal ridge and her second and third fingers just below it. She applies pronounced pressure until the urge to ejaculate recedes. After several moments they repeat this procedure, attempting to lengthen the periods of stimulation before she applies the pressure. After improvement in control satisfactory to both spouses, intercourse is attempted with the wife in a position where she can again readily apply the needed pressure if her husband senses imminent premature ejaculation. They continue this program until the husband has established enough control to be able to feel sufficiently in control of his ejaculation to please both himself and his wife.

This method is quite different from previous ones. Some were told to reduce the stimulation to the penis by physical means such as using an anesthetic ointment on the glans, putting a condom over the penis, biting the inner side of one's cheek to cause enough discomfort to be distracting, or leaving all the clothes on to cut down on body sensation. Cognitive gambits were also suggested which would lessen some of the emotional stimulation. These might consist of reciting the multiplication tables, replaying a golf game, or mentally solving an algebra problem.

Employing such distracting techniques can only defraud the couple out of the very sensation they lovingly wish to provide for one another as well as detract from their emotional intimacy.

B. Retarded Ejaculation: Although this condition does not occur frequently, it should be mentioned here. In this situation the husband finds it difficult or impossible to ejaculate while his penis is in the vagina, even with sufficient stimulation and with long periods of vigorous thrusting. In some cases he may be able to be stimulated to orgasm outside the vagina. This may be a primary condition in which he has always had this problem; or it may be a secondary, later development. In some cases it is first noted after some deep emotional trauma. And in some cases it may be that, though able to erect, a man has never been able to ejaculate.

Some psychologists feel that this condition is emotionally triggered almost entirely. Anger at a spouse can consciously or unconsciously suppress ejaculation. It may also be "punishment" for a perceived infidelity on the wife's part. Sometimes a deep-seated, perhaps unconscious fear of impregnating his wife can be involved. Among other possible causes, these thought processes have been explored in working with affected individuals. So far no clear-cut or definitive therapeutic approach has been established. When the problem persists, psychotherapeutic intervention is indicated.

III. Erectile Problems

The term "impotent" has been used to describe a man's inability to achieve and maintain an erection sufficient for penetration in sexual intercourse. This term also has negative connotations and is being replaced. Given the great importance most men place on their sexual ability, the negative images which the word brings to mind (i.e., powerlessness, ineffectiveness, helplessness) were defeating and disabling in themselves. Anything that decreases a man's appreciation of his powers—even a term—can have undesireable effects.

At this time psychologists recognize several types of erectile problems. Some types have physical causes—an anatomical defect or injury either to the nervous or the reproductive system. These, however, are quite rare. Other erectile problems derive from such disease conditions as diabetes, anemia, hypothyroidism, malnutrition, or any other condition which effects one's health and vigor generally. Diseases of the prostate gland may also be responsible for an inability to erect.

Drugs (and some of these may be prescription drugs essential for treatment of other functional diseases), opiates, and alcohol can also be the culprits. So important is this that sometimes the physician will ask the patient to be drug free for thirty days prior to a sexual evaluation examination.

But by far the greater number of men, evaluated by some at up to 85 percent of the cases of erectile disability, are affected by psychological factors. Emotional inhibitions or problems seem to interfere with impulses to the brain. These impulses in turn act on nervous centers of the spinal cord controlling erection.

Erectile dysfunction has been divided into two categories: primary, for men who have never had an erection; and secondary for men who at one time have been sexually functional but at some point have ceased being able to have an erection firm enough to penetrate or have become unable to maintain erection within the vagina for a sufficient length of time to bring on ejaculation. Masters and Johnson reserve the term *dysfunction* for a man who fails to erect when adequately stimulated in up to 25 percent of his sexual attempts.

As with premature ejaculation, retarded ejaculation can result when one or two unsuccessful attempts at intercourse may become so threatening that the anxiety progression takes over and a man can worry himself into a chronic condition. Most men at times suffer depression under the weight of staggering bills, feel self-devalued over a missed promotion, or become preoccupied with an important business deal. If a man is prepared for the possibility that his sexual functioning will be less notable at times, he can better accept its happening, then, without a premonition of doom. Should he be taking a medication or be diagnosed as having a disease which may contribute to erectile problems, he should remember that these factors do not invariably cause such problems. Concerned over whether he will be sexually affected by them and concentrating mightily to monitor his next erection, he can bring enough stress upon himself actually to bring about what he fears. How much more rewarding to enter into lovemaking moments without an agenda which demands measuring up to some ideal performance. Men with this problem need to learn to relax, enjoy, and experience.

Once again, the wife's part in the problem can be substantial. If she is perceived as demanding, disappointed, disgusted, passive, impatient, or bored, his problem will compound. I wish to reemphasize interpersonal relationship here as basic to alleviating the husband's distress.

Together the couple should explore ways to enhance sexual arousal through body touch. They should do this in the way described for a woman's pleasure. During this time, while his wife is caressing him, he can relax and attend to his own body feelings. At no point is erection or ejaculation the goal. He simply learns to enjoy sustained stimulation without demand. He can be assured that when he loses his fear and anxiety, intromission will eventually result spontaneously in ejaculation.

Since emotional factors play such a large part in contributing to the problem, the interpersonal aspects have a greater chance of satisfactory resolution with the services of a counselor. This would always be true of primary dysfunction and more than likely true also of long-standing problems.

Many men have great difficulty even considering counseling assistance in an area so threatening, so integral to self-concept. It will never be easy. But recently large strides have been made in the treatment of sexual dysfunction. Therapists, physicians, and counselors have learned skills of relating that greatly relieve the tension that people feel on their first visit. Generally that initial appointment will cut through much anxiety and will often bring a sense of relief with the knowledge that there is a competent professional who is able to understand and deal with the problem.

In Marriage Only?

That's one question that Adam and Eve in the Garden of Eden never had! In this primal situation no question existed about waiting to express their sexual feelings until after marriage. Yet this is a real problem for many unmarried people in a day when the term "meaningful relationships" usually implies a complete sexual experience. Since statistics are so variable and outdated so quickly, I believe that it would serve little purpose here to record figures on how many people of varied age groups admit sexual intercourse before marriage. Nor would these figures give us a life-warm picture of the concern, ambivalence, hurt and stress so often reported with premarital sexual experimentation.

I am distressed that we have not been successful in making premarital chastity a more attractive option to young people. But then I am not sure that my generation, as parents, and the ones before have done a very good job of making the whole marriage package winsome. Counselors' offices are visited by many young people who do not have pleasant memories of what went on in their parents' homes. They often recall arguing, bickering, hostility, and intolerance. They seldom recall loving words, hugging, kissing, and other touching between their parents. They report little or no outward evidence of a loving relationship. Parents' sexuality was so well hidden that the young counselees found it almost impossible to imagine that marital sexual expression went on between their parents, at least from the day of their own conception onward.

Now, let's explore this matter of premarital sexuality together. I am suggesting that we do this in two parts, dividing the two groups of unmarried persons into teenagers and adults.

Sex and Teenagers

Anyone who longs to be a "carefree teenager" again probably has a poor memory. Many developmental tasks must be worked through at this time. Not the least of these is the realizing one's own sexual identity and coming to terms with it. From the first pubescent realization that the opposite sex suddenly is less opposite than interesting, tensions and urgencies are daily companions. A new physical body evolves, with the necessity for accepting the changes but without the ability to alter perceived imperfections which now become significant. How can you approve of yourself if your hair is too curly or too straight? Your nose is too long or too flat? Your stature is too tall or too short? This is not to mention sexual changes which cause embarrassment, worry, and bewilderment—particularly when they have not been anticipated and discussed with open, concerned parents. About this time society catapults these unprepared young people into dating relationships.

Now, dating can make solid contributions to growing up. It can help young people to learn how to communicate and get along with opposite-sex peers. Dating experiences can help them to sort out and understand why they appreciate some people and avoid others. They learn to recognize those whom they "hit it off with," those they feel enhanced by, and those who seem to diminish their good feelings about themselves. Dating can provide an enriching experience when it encompasses exploration of ideas, hobbies, sports, music, nature, etc. It can also be the vehicle in which young persons learn to understand and act responsibly on the newly discovered sexual feelings that they are experiencing. But when dating becomes confining, when it is used for conquest or even manipulation, it is not a positive force.

Parents are frequently concerned about their young people getting into dating, fearing that it might push them into sexual experimentation. Indeed some teenagers are more likely to follow this pattern. Young people who feel a lack of warmth and caring in family relationships may fall within this group. They long for a place where they feel accepted and cherished, even though they may be giving out "vibes" of wanting to be left alone and not "made over."

For nearly two years I worked with a group of young girls, ages thirteen to nineteen, in various stages of pregnancy. Over and over again they expressed feelings of not being held dear by their parents. Verbatim exerpts of some of our conversations include the following: "I can't remember either of my parents telling me that they love me." "I get yelled at a lot." "It seems that nothing I do is right." "My parents are real good at telling me what I do wrong but never say anything when I do it right." "We never talk things over quietly." "I never really felt that I mattered much to either of my parents."

It can follow, then, that when a teenage girl has a poor self-image, it is easier for her to get into a sexual situation which promises good feelings, however fleeting. The person who feels insecure and unsure is less apt to be able to withstand peer pressure which insist, "*Everybody's* doing it—and if you don't, you're really behind the times."

Incidentally, the good news is that everyone is *not* doing it. A nationwide poll conducted among 21,000 juniors and seniors in a recent edition of *Who's Who of American High School Students* found that 76 percent had not had sexual intercourse and 81 percent of these were linked to organized religion. The poll showed that 60 percent intended to remain virgin until they were married, and 50 percent said they would not live with someone prior to marriage.

This brings us to the next point. Young people who have no firm, clear-cut goals in life or who are not serious about these goals, as well as those not established in a religious conviction of their own, are more likely to get into sexual experiences. Well over half of these young people above said that their religious beliefs played an important part in their moral standards and in their actions.

One further group of young people seen as vulnerable to sexual activity are those who have not learned to defer gratification until a more apropriate (i.e., healthful, morally sound, economically wise) time. Children who have never been required to wait for a cherished object or experience are done a disfavor by parents who long to give their offspring "opportunities and things I never had." The young are deprived of the joy of anticipation—working toward while doing without. "Wait" can be a good four-letter word.

Frequently young people ask, "When you're *really* in love, isn't it OK?" This question calls for an exploration of what love is. Perhaps we can first state what love is *not!* Love should not be confused with a pounding heart. Not too long ago, a highway patrolman stopped me on the freeway to point out my infringement of a traffic law. Believe me, my heart was literally pounding when his blinking red light and siren pulled me over to the side of the road; but I was not the least bit "in love" with him (even though I am glad to report that he did not give me a ticket!)

Nor is love "feeling good all over." If someone were to present me with a check for a million dollars today, I would "feel very good all over"—but that feeling would be no indication of my love toward the generous (and unfortunately mythical) donor.

Love doesn't mean that you "just couldn't do without" the person. There are many people that you couldn't do without. There is mother (who cooks, washes your clothes, and keeps house). There is father (who pays the bills). There are certain teachers (who prepare you for passing to the next grade). And let's not forget the gas station operator! Nor should being in love be confused with a natural need for cherishing and caring. Sometimes sexual feelings can be mistaken for love, when in fact they are simply widespread and normal feelings indicating that a young person is only coming to an age when she or he can learn to be responsible for these feelings but is not ready yet to demonstrate them.

How, then, does one recognize love? It seems to me that real love is outgoing and not self-centered. Rather than causing one to think "What's in it for me?" ("He's neat looking" or "When I'm with her the other guys really notice"), real love entertains ideas of what it can contribute to the well-being and happiness of someone else. A couple truly in love doesn't exclude others and want to be alone constantly, but wishes at times to share and include others—such as peers and parents. People in love will be happy to share their company, ideas, time, and values. A person in love wants to hear all about the other person, for communication through talking is pleasurable and valuable. He wishes to explore the other's childhood, family, school experiences, and philosophies. This is not a dull, dry exercise but is full of surprises and incidents which sometimes delight the hearer, sometimes sadden, but always enrich feelings for one another.

People who are in love should be more energetic, more creative than before. They should be able to study harder, work harder, and accomplish more. Loving also includes liking and respecting. It approves of or allows for the habits, personalities, and interests of the other. There is no hidden agenda of wanting to effect major changes in the other to make him or her more acceptable, more "fitting" the fantasized image of the "perfect love." Love does not try to "talk into" or coerce, rationalize, or manipulate the other's values or ideals. Love seeks the ultimate and constant good of the loved one.

These concepts are difficult for a teenager to understand. Yet perhaps this youthful inability to understand may be one of the best reasons for responsible adults to advise against sexual experience for the immature, though eager, teenager. She or he is simply not yet capable of mature love.

But teenagers generally want to know *specifically* why isn't it OK. When I was a teenager, the specific answer to that specific question was usually "You might get pregnant," or "What if you get a social disease?" or the clincher, "The Bible says you shouldn't."

Now, while I subscribe to the former two reasons, I don't believe them to be the only important considerations. To discount the hurt and the broken lives that go with these would indeed be shortsighted. But sophisticated teenagers can avoid pregnanacies, with the help of physicians and free clinics, and most cases of veneral disease do respond to medical treatment. These arguments have thus lost much of their persuasive force. We may have made them the main reason to give our teenagers in order to induce them to refrain from sexual intercourse, but we now have to trade those dire threats for thoughtful consideration.

I also am committed to the concept behind the reminder "The Bible says you shouldn't." I am not sure, however, that this is how God appreciates being understood. The Author of the Book invites, "Come now, let us reason together." Isaiah 1:18, RSV.

Let us set down some of the reasons why I feel that sexual experience for teenagers is not in keeping with God's plan for lifelong happy, healthy sexuality. The first sexual experience for a girl is generally extremely significant. If it turns out to be disappointing or disillusioning, it can cast a long shadow on future adjustment. The event is so often associated with furtiveness, fear, and speed—none of which teaches tenderness, carefulness, and concern. This falls far short of the ideal setting of commitment, understanding, and approval. My mind goes back to the ancient Hebrew custom of bringing the bride into the mother's tent for the nuptial experience. This was not a secret, hurried event but a celebration to be joyously and proudly experienced. What an auspicious beginning!

Motivation behind sexual activity between two teenagers is usually different for each. A boy may engage as a means of bolstering his masculinity and enhancing his ego. Sometimes his peers indoctrinate him into believing that sexual activity is necessary to prove his manhood—a notch on his belt. A girl may engage out of a fear of being rejected if unwilling, not only by the boy involved but often also by her same-sex peers. Because sexual experience signifies the closest bond which can exist between a female and a male, when a teenage couple enters it with separate agendas, the result cannot be expected to be the most fulfilling and joyous.

My counseling experience has proven to me that when two young people begin physical touching, they usually do not realize the progressive aspect of the tensions involved. Petting and loving with tender verbal interchanges usually prepares the participants physically and emotionally for sexual intercourse and climax. Teenagers, who are not yet able to understand this bonding process, can go through a series of sexual exchanges without realizing the beauty and impact of each stage. The joys of holding hands becomes but a preliminary to further touching rather than a warm and wonderful experience in itself. Many dates could pass where hand holding is the only touching activity—exploring the nuances of feelings involved in the good aspects of this experience. Watch couples of any age, and note how often they are observed in this precious activity. For teenagers to use this early physical expression of fondness as merely a stepping-stone to the next level of intimacy is to unwittingly cheat themselves out of a truly significant experience.

It may not seem pertinent, in this day of eliminating the "double standard" for female and male sexual behavior, or to talk of "losing respect." But I must confess that I read and hear more of this double standard's being erased than I observe. We cannot underestimate the power of cultural, societal and spiritual controls even in the face of escalating permissiveness. Yes, boys still do admit losing respect for a girl who agrees to intercourse.

How often young women I have counseled have impressed this upon my consciousness. They discussed their boyfriends' pleas for sex and the assurance they received that they would not "think less" of them.

However, faced with their girl friends' pregnancies, they begin to question: "How many other fellows have you done this with?" "If you would do it with me, why wouldn't you do it with others?"

As I read the literature on premarital sexual intercourse, I find that my opinion echoes others in the field. In the May 1979 *Medical Aspects of Human Sexuality* four hundred psychiatrists were polled on the question of premarital sex and the teenager. Interesting concepts came from the poll. Among them was the opinion that teenage boys still distinguish between "good" girls who won't engage in sex and "bad" girls who will: "The majority of psychiatrists still believe, in keeping with the double standard of morality, that most boys still classify girls as 'good' or 'bad' depending on whether or not they are virginal. Data indicates that there has been a decrease in this classical attitude of boys. This double standard is true of not only middle-class boys but boys in lower and working class populations."

I decry a system which holds that boys may act on their sexual urges—"boys will be boys"—while girls who do are branded "bad." Since our population is pretty well divided between males and females percentagewise, I am not sure where these judgmental young men expect to find virgins while they are busily deflowering them! But it is important for girls to be aware of this lingering attitude. Perhaps they need to make some demands for virginity in the young men that they see as potential mates. The double standard can be erased in two ways: by both men and women willingly accepting premarital intercourse in either partner, or by both men and women demanding abstinence before marriage. I see greater gains in the latter way.

Some other interesting concepts that came from the survey mentioned above are as follows: The majority of psychiatrists believe that sexual experience has a negative effect on the teenager's personality. Middle-class girls still feel guilt about their sexual feelings and behavior. The majority of teenagers are not capable of making a mature decision about whether to engage in sexual relationships.

I was interested recently in the quotation by Alton in the *American Journal of Orthopsychiatry* (April 9, 1977) which stated: "Too early, immature sexual relationships may harm the development of love feelings. Sex life at an early age often has its roots in emotional distress and seeks to compensate for loneliness, disturbed relationships with parents, or inferiority feelings, or it reflects the desire to gain prestige by proving one's manliness or womanliness." My clinical experience had led me to the same conclusion; so I decided to explore this point further. The following question concerned me particularly: Can engaging in sex at too early an age impair the ability to subsequently have a good sexual experience? I have counseled with women in their twenties and thirties who began sexual intercourse in their early teens. Now they are concerned because they sense no pleasure in sexual experience, though they may be married to a loving and helpful partner. I have pondered much about this and have tried to find something in the literature beyond the physical reasons for restricting pregnancy in a teenage girl. (We have already discussed the fear of pregnancy and danger of venereal disease. We should also mention the greater incidence of cervical cancer with early and promiscuous sexual intercourse.) Are there ages when sexual intercourse can have completely negative effects on later aspects of a woman's sexual experience?

Erik Erikson in his widely accepted eight developmental stages of man has suggested that each developmental stage has certain tasks which need to be at least partially accomplished before the next can be successfully attempted (See *Childhood and Society*, pp. 261-263). He categorizes adolescence as the identity stage, when a firm sense of self should be developed. The next stage, young adulthood, is designated as the stage of intimacy. This is the stage of giving and receiving good experience. Erikson posits that without a rudimentary identity there is nothing to give or receive.

Following up on this premise, Dr. William Patrick states: "At this present time however this arrangement seems to be in the process of reversal; for many youngsters, sexual intimacy now comes long before identity is established. But when intimacy precedes identity, the intimacy tends to be of a spurious nature—lovemaking without love. Because there is no firm sense of self or self-definition as a base for intimacy, this reversal process necessarily leads to a tentative, noncommittal approach to relationships."—*Medical Aspects of Human Sexuality*, Oct. 19, 1976, pp. 39, 40. He further states that recent studies at Yale University Health Center indicate that adolescents who engage in early and frequent sexual experiences have great difficulty in later obtaining a capacity for a deep intimacy in which giving and trusting is required. I now believe this to be the problem that some of my patients with sexual dysfunction are experiencing. A "tentative, non-committal approach" to sex is not the kind of relationship which yields a "knowing" of the other, a deep understanding of the lover enhanced and completed by a giving and openness. This experience cannot be anticipated or even imagined by two adolescents battling for a sense of self-identity. A pair of youngsters fumbling with one another's genitals is as far from God's ideals of "the two shall be one" as a two year old's smudged finger painting is from a Renoir canvas.

At the present time and in the main these deficit effects are seen only in women. I believe that this may stem from the fact that the female emotions are more deeply affected by teenage sexual experiences. This idea has been captured in the adage, "Boys give love to get sex; girls give sex to get love."

Now I have a lot of respect for, and confidence in, young men. My experience has shown me that they generally are sincere in feeling that casual sex isn't "all that bad." I do not believe that they want to hurt another person in the pursuit of their own momentary desires. I am confident that if they understood that having a sexual experience with a girl could be an incident that would deprive her of full enjoyment of her sexuality in future years, when they may long since have erased the incident from mind, they would carefully consider their part in the drama. No responsible individual would deliberately be the perpetrator of such tragedy. And I fully believe that teenagers are able to comprehend that concept.

Let us discuss now some suggestions for handling this problem which looms so large before teenagers. In a world in which we are daily flooded with sexually oriented material—a true multimedia approach—it becomes necessary to plan. I should mention that more and more young men are reporting being pressured for sexual activity by their girl friends. I don't want to give the impression that all the urging is on the part of the male, for this simply isn't true.

At first I would suggest that each teenager gain a healthy respect for the insistencies of the sexual drive. Well in advance one must decide coolly and logically what to do about kissing, necking, petting, and intercourse. No one can provide a checklist of dos and don'ts which is appropriate under all circumstances. Sometimes a fleeting touch or a reaching for hands can be as provocative as a caress. A bear hug can be less erotic than reaching for a hand. To ask if it is all right to kiss may be like asking if it is all right to eat. What do you mean by "kiss"? A brush against the forehead or cheek? A perfunctory "smack"? A lingering union of the lips? Further, what does the action indicate—this kiss, this caress, this hug? What happens to the emotional and physical system when it is experienced? What would be the result of carrying on further, right now, with these feelings? Perhaps we can say that the demonstration of affection becomes questionable when it turns your thoughts and actions away from what you should be doing, thinking, and valuing to what you decided in advance that you do not want to become part of your Christian conduct at this point in your life.

In keeping with this conscious decision, then, it is only prudent to avoid situations loaded with sexual stimuli—i.e., erotic reading or viewing, being alone for long periods of time with no constructive activity planned ("parking," etc.). Participating in groups and planning creatively for interesting and absorbing projects would probably avoid much "petting by default"—simply because there is nothing else to do. Many times teenagers are bored into sexual events.

Young people need to cultivate ways of demonstrating their fondness for one another other than physical expression. I can think right now of several: cooking or otherwise creating special treats for one another, bringing books from the library and reading together, cutting out items of interest from magazines and newspapers to share with one another, or starting a scrapbook in an area of special interest.

Further, I advise young people to plan their responses to a suggestion for sexual contact. I suggest that these be written out in advance so that there will be no question about their being imprinted on the mind. Young people have told me that this has helped them invaluably. Here are several suggestions that teenagers have used and/or have told me about:

"Look, I really like you and enjoy being with you, and I don't want to spoil that feeling."

"The way I feel about intimacy now, I would really regret doing something that doesn't feel right for me."

"I am really trying to be careful about physical commitment, and I have a feeling that you are the kind of person that I can trust to help me with that."

"There are many things that I don't know about you as a person; I would rather get acquainted with you."

"That's really not me, and I want very much to be the me I have decided to be, and I guess that I really need your help."

"I'm not ready for that yet; I have too many big plans. I bet you do too."

"I know that I would be disappointed in myself, and I think that I know you well enough to know that you wouldn't want that."

"You know, I don't think you prove love that way. I think love is helping the other person to be the person that he wants to be."

"If you really love me, you won't pressure me into doing something that I am not ready for yet."

"I wish that you wouldn't do that. It makes me feel uncomfortable being with you, and I know that you won't want me to feel that way."

"I've made some pretty big decisions about that part of my life, and I am going to ask you to help me stay by them. OK?

Often when I have talked to groups of young people on these issues, during question-and-answer periods I invariably have several questioners who I sense are deeply distressed. They ask in words that approximate these: "I have already had sex with my boyfriend/girlfriend, and I don't feel it's right. What can I do now?" "I have been sexually active; does that mean I'm doomed?"

Well, that's the bad news, and here is the good. Praise God you can be a new person in Christ Jesus with new desires, new values, and a new beginning. The same God that forgives us for not correctly demonstrating His love offers His robe of righteousness to cancel this impurity.

I was interested in reading an article by Arlene and Joel Moskowitz (*Medical Aspects of Human Sexuality*, December, 1975) which recorded the use of the term "secondary virginity." This phrase signifies young persons who, after a period of "disillusioning sexual activity," choose to remain "chaste" from this point until marriage. They state that this decision is linked with their desire to establish a sexual relationship that includes commitment.

But as a Christian I believe that we have the right to speak of the same concept in even more liberating terms. I like the phrase "spiritual revirgination." If I read correctly, this is what God offers to people who have erred in this respect:

"I will forgive their iniquity, and I will remember their sin [sexual or otherwise] no more." Jeremiah 31:34.

"He [God] will have compassion upon us and . . . cast all their sins into the depths of the sea." Micah 7:19.

"As far as the east is from the west, so far has he removed our transgressions from us." Psalm 103:12, NIV.

God's forgiveness is immediate and complete. It now remains for the guilty person to accept that forgiveness and to forgive himself or herself.

We seem to have created a hierarchy for sins, and we tend to put sexual sins at the top of the list. We are told by inspiration that the sins of selfishness and self-satisfaction are the most difficult to deal with. And these attributes can well be part of the character of someone who might be totally aghast at the idea of sexual misdeeds. The same Christ who holds out this compassionate gift of "spiritual revirgination" was also once a teenager. Unlike Adam, who could not have understood the problems involved, Christ can. Teenagers need to feel that He is "in there" trying to help them, not waiting to pass judgment.

I found this poem in my files. While the author's name is known, the source is not. So without being able to ask permission, I hope that the author will be pleased to have her efforts shared with teen-agers.

A Teenager's Prayer

Walk with me, Christ!
I wonder—what was it like when You were
young?
Was there an "in" crowd at Nazareth?
Were You on the fringe, just watching?

Did You walk alone
through the springtime's glory?

Did You know the loneliness of being
different?

Did You run down the hilly slopes
filled with joy at just being alive?
Was the whole world brilliantly,
beautifully, waiting for You?

Did You know of the choices You had to
make?

Walk with me, Jesus!

The world is waiting for me.
I'm on the brink of many choices
  and decisions;
Walk with me, Christ!

Life is fresh and tender and new—
I can feel the future approaching.

Lord, help me to keep the whiteness of
  my soul.

—Patricia Halbe

Sex and Unmarried Adults

While a chorus of secular voices still rises against the physical and emotional appropriateness of sex for teenagers, this chorus shrinks to a small ensemble when we speak of sex between two consenting adults before marriage. More and more religious bodies are being tolerant of sex within a "meaningful relationship." The former religious proscriptions are weakening. Life-styles in this area include those living alone and having sexual expression on a random basis, those living alone but reserving sexual access to only one other person, and couples "living together." Each of these groups seems to be growing. In reference to couples living together, the Census Bureau has just released a report for 1979 indicating 1.1 million "illicit" (the Bureau's term) couples. The sharpest rise in those adopting this life-style occurs in the under twenty-five-year-old category.

Several factors underlie the growing numbers of unmarried adults seeking sexual congress. One hears with increasing frequency, "But it seems so right; it feels so good; I enjoy it!"

And since we are living in a hedonistic society where feelings are often made the adopted norm, this attitude should not surprise us. Expressions such as "my thing," "doing it my way" and "it has to be me" punctuate our conversations in this self-oriented "me" society. We think less in terms of community where we are our "brother's [or sister's] keeper." The Christian ethic of assuming compassionate responsibility for others seems passé. A British quaker group says, Each partner of "the sexually-involved couple should be committed to the other—should be open to the other in heart and mind. This would mean that each cared deeply what might happen to the other and would do everything possible to meet the other's need and lessen any suffering that had to be faced. It would mean a willingness to accept responsibility and some fore-knowledge of what responsibility is involved. . . . Whenever there is a deliberate intention to avoid responsibility in all possibility of being involved and committed, then evil creeps in and the act becomes mutual exploitation."

I propose that marriage *is* this act of commitment and that reaching for marital sexual intimacy without the benefit of a solemnization of marriage promises is an indication of uncertainty. To enter into an act of communication so deeply significant as sexual union in a state of uncertainty is to miss it's greatest import—its symbolization of Christ's tender regard and love for His church, a love which is unchanging and irrevocable.

Let us also consider the factor of the need for intimacy, belonging, and togetherness. Our culture, which consists almost entirely of nuclear families and one-person living units, is lonely—starving for a tender touch, for a symbol of being cherished. We have sometimes mistaken physical intimacy for complete intimacy. Real intimacy involves two people coming close together by exploring thoughts, feelings, ideas, and values. This kind of intimacy is not as easily achieved as going to bed together. Unfortunately, many people substitute the latter for the former in their eagerness to be "involved." Some of the loneliest most unfulfilled people in the world are sharing their genitals in the desperate hope of finding intimacy.

For others, sexual expression is a way of winning approval. In order to feel more attractive, to enhance their self-image, they engage in sex. And it can bring brief reassurance from the stress of a feeling of inadequacy. But it rarely lasts long. Such persons follow "conquest" after "conquest" to reproduce the good feeling.

Many see sex now taking on a recreational quality—"fun and games." The "games" idea implies competition. The rule book or sex manual becomes important, with many of these becoming springboards for seeing sexual expression as a set of techniques; the "winner" is the one who can excel in physical prowess. Richard F. Hetlinger, counselor and faculty member of Kenyon College, states, "On what grounds does one expect to make an untroubled shift from sex as fun, to sex as a means of expressing love in marriage? Does one expect the particular habits of emotional and bodily response which now regulate the sexual responsiveness to be easily transformed to the emotional and physical expectations of the married partner?"

Sex is also employed as a weapon by which to manifest hostility, contempt, or anger. We need not enlarge upon this concept here.

We must spend some time, however, considering the notion of sex as a means of eliciting love. More than a few people engage in sex because they feel that it will increase their chances of "falling in love." But sex in itself rarely kindles a deep love relationship. If it did, can you imagine the innumerable choices that a prostitute would have!

While marriage, by way of pregnancy, can result from premarital sex, few people in this situation see this as ideal. In this area, if one seeks diligently enough, one can find a study to

8—T.F.E.

show almost anything one wishes. Here are some examples: "Premarital sex leads to poor marital adjustment," "It leads to better marital adjustment." "Premarital sex dissipates love." "It strengthens love." However, a number of researchers have reported that women who have had premarital intercourse are more than two times as likely to commit adultery after marriage. And several studies done by well-respected behavioral scientists in the 1950s agree that overall marital adjustment of those who enter marriage with no premarital sexual experience tends to be higher and they are least likely to undergo divorce later (Truman, 1938; Locke, 1951; Burgess and Wall, 1953). This concept has been corroborated in 1975 at the Ohio State University.

I have made it a habit to ask couples who have come from counseling, and who in the course of their social histories have reported premarital sexual experience, whether they feel that it had strengthened their relationship and if they would repeat the same pattern if they could relive this part of their lives. Some have expressed rather neutral feelings on the subject, but for the most part one or both of the spouses has indicated feeling that it would have been better for their marriage if they had waited. Some of the reasons they gave are as follows;

"It's been hard for me to trust my mate—I keep wondering if there were others."

"Once we got into sex, we quit talking to one another and did not explore some of the important areas that have since become points of conflict."

"I wouldn't have married at all if we hadn't gotten into sex. I would have broken up with my fiancé, since we were arguing so much and really weren't compatible. I figured that once we were into sex it was too late to break up; we were obligated."

"I feel manipulated now when I think of the reasons my boyfriend gave me for having sex before marriage."

"Premarital sex is really no preparation for marital sex. The situations just are not the same."

"I think my problem with sex began with the first sexual experience, which was connected with so much guilt and misinformation that it conditioned me wrongly."

In speaking with unmarried women who are engaged in premarital sexual activity—some randomly, some seriously—I find them generally a somewhat uneasy, troubled group. Since many of them do not claim religious convictions, their tensions cannot be completely attributed to guilt feelings. Some assure me that they have good *physical* feelings. But I do not get the feeling of unalloyed pleasure, fulfillment, and delight, in spite of the feeling of independence from the norms by which they were reared and now reject. They are passively or actively engaged in sexual intercourse without the "highs" that they expected, even though they may have sensitive partners.

I wonder if this lack of full satisfaction is not because sexual expression was meant to be more than physical release and was intended to be enriched by emotional, social, and spiritual components. I am reminded of the words of Dr. Mary Calderone, director of Sex Education and Information Council of the United States, "Every time you have intercourse with another person, you reduce the significance and the quality of the act as a bond linking you exclusively with one person. . . . How many times and how casually are you willing to invest a portion of a total self and be the custodian of a life investment of the other person without the assurance that these investments are made for keeps?"

I also have a deep concern for those persons who are sexually active because of peer pressure. The problem is so great that some virgins even experience guilt and shame when so many around them are sexually active. Many times they are made to feel abnormal, inhibited, or even neurotic for not being able to go along with their peers. More than one case on record reveals that women have sought to have their hymens surgically incised. They felt that this would protect them from being thought "freaky" or "deviant" if detected virgins. This is a tyrannical imposition. It seems a mockery of the so-called "freedom" that sexually active unmarrieds feel that they enjoy by not following "outdated" societal norms. Yet they feel free to impose the slavery of their choices on others—the slavery of being forced into decisions against one's own values for fear of contempt. I have a cartoon by Mary Gauerka in my files which expresses this thought. It shows two women walking on the street, one saying to the other, "If it is wrong for me to impose my morality on others, why is it all right for them to impose their immorality on me!"

If I had but one brief moment to speak to the whole world of sexually uninvolved young adults, I would ask them to stop being a silent majority. They need to be as vocal in extolling the freedom of chastity—freedom from emotional and physical trauma, freedom from feeling guilt, freedom from losing self-respect. We know that *not* everyone is doing it. Let us hear from you!

Often I hear couples say that they felt that premarital sex was important to find out if they were sexually compatible. There is rarely such a thing as sexual physical incompatibility. Less than 5 percent of sexual dysfunction between husband and wife is caused by physical problems; even a smaller precentage has anything to do with organ size or penis acceptance by the vagina. God took care of that by creating genital organs which, through elasticity, natural lubrication, and flexibility could accommodate one another. Emotional aspects are almost entirely responsible for sexual problems.

Again, I hear couples talk about the need to reduce the sexual tensions that are aroused by their being together so near to the anticipated wedding experience. Well, it is mutually comforting that no one has ever become ill or deceased as a result of not surrendering to sexual tension. Dr. Elaine Pierson has aptly entitled her book *Sex Is Never an Emergency!* The many married couples who live fruitful, productive lives without having had sexual experiences before their marriage attest to that. But later conflicts have been instituted by resentments of the spouse who exerted pressure on the other to engage in sexual expression prematurely. Generally the "yielder" is the one with the least power, and manipulative power plays are not the basis upon which to build good marriages.

"That little piece of paper doesn't mean anything!" You've heard it, I know. It is true; most of us who have been married for a number of years probably don't know where that piece of paper is now without some searching of drawers and files. But that small document *stands* for many things. It stands for commitment—not "till you displease me" or "till we have irreconcilable differences" but "till death do us part." It stands for a commitment to work through problems, to stubbornly build, from tensions and conflicts, a strong, dependable union. A man and woman who experience sexual changes through the years learn to understand and appreciate one anothers' sensitivities, needs, and rhythms. This "little piece of paper" indicates that you have stated in front of God and other people your intention to be faithful to your marriage vows. It indicates that you have invoked legal powers to acknowledge your commitment and that you have invited God's church and His ministers to sanction in a very special way what you are promising to one another at this time. Hereafter, God, your friends, your parents, and the entire church community are bound together in pledging to this new social unit acceptance and support of its vows.

Forsaking All Others

We live in a culture of conundrums. Adult Americans condemn unfaithfulness to marriage vows, and yet it seems almost an accepted part of our social system at this time. In 1977 the National Opinion Research Center at the University of Chicago asked a representative national sample of persons of age eighteen and over: "What is your opinion about a married person having sexual relations with someone other than the marriage partner—is it always wrong, almost always wrong, wrong only sometimes, or not wrong at all?" Of those questioned 73 percent said "always wrong," and another 14 percent said "almost always wrong." Only 3 percent said "not wrong at all."

In this same survery, respondents expressed a different attitude toward premarital sex and represented a softening of judgmental attitudes. The so-called "sexual revolution," then, seems to have passed over the married couple, in theory.

In spite of this unexpected endorsement for marital fidelity, statistics indicate that in practice fidelity is less and less the norm. The literature is replete with statements by authors from almost any named discipline which discuss extramarital sex using such terms as "unimportant," "understandable," "normal," "justifiable," "meaningful," and even "therapeutic."

Reasons for engaging in this activity are thought to be

numerous, and aside from prolonged separation, illness, and physical dysfunction, they include such prodromes as disappointment, lack of interest of one spouse, depression, desire to seek refuge from the conflict of a troubled marriage, revolt against societal norms, wish to punish one's spouse (or self), impulsivity, jealousy, boredom, effort to ensure proof of femininity or masculinity, retaliation, curiosity, and social pressure.

Dissatisfaction with marriage can cause one or both of the spouses to turn into other variations of sexual expression. One of these is the open-marriage concept. The book *Open Marriage,* authored by Nena O'Neil and her husband, George, reported salutary effects achieved by going outside of marriage for sexual experience. The best seller suggested that the harmful aspect of extramarital sex was the usual deviousness and secretiveness that characterized it. The implications were that if a couple could accept this need in one another and be open about it, the experience could be a positive one. Nena O'Neil has since somewhat amended that theory.

The follow-up (of the couples quoted in *Open Marriage* as being enthusiastic about extra-marital experiences) shows that they have not been able to maintain long-term marriages while engaged in that activity. A two-year period was as long as any marriage in the original study could cope with this openness. In an interview in the *New York Times,* October 1977, Mrs. O'Neil stated, "The assurance of sexual fidelity is still an important and necessary attribute of most marriages." And her new book, *The Marriage Premise,* has some very warm and positive things to say about marital fidelity.

Another variation in sexual styles among the married is "swinging," in which sexual pleasure may be taken whenever and wherever and however it is found. Drs. William Masters and Virginia Johnson, in their book *The Pleasure Bond: A New Look at Sexuality and Commitment,* conducted a symposium for four couples and one trio engaged in "swinging." After talking at some length with them, the researchers seemed convinced that what the participants were feeling was not sexual intimacy but sexual consciousness. Let me quote briefly from this book:

"In fact, what the individuals in the symposium were suggesting is a false similarity—a physical interchange is not an emotional interchange, and physical intimacy is not the same as emotional intimacy. Neither physical interchange nor physical intimacy is a sound basis for continuing a relationship. Anyone who suggests that intercourse is in itself a good foundation, proves, with that single statement, an ignorance of two different relationships: such a person knows nothing of the meaning of sex in the context of emotional involvement, and such a person knows nothing of the meaning of friendship, neither of its origins nor how it is developed nor the part that it can play in the lives of any two individuals."

After one year Masters and Johnson met again with the same group and discovered that of those mentioned, one couple was divorced, two couples had stopped swinging; and of the trio, one member had departed to "search for her own identity." In the above book a chapter titled "What Sexual Fidelity Means in a Marriage" has some very hearty things to say about the promise of sexual fidelity. It concludes with these important words:

"As couples, the question that they want answered, is not what makes extra-marital sex right or wrong . . . but what makes it unnecessary. The answer that they need is not one that preaches the moral virtues of commitment and fidelity but one that translates these values into functional terms that examine how and why the sense of being mutually committed may contribute to the sexual response of both partners and to the endurability of this exclusive relationship."

Dr. Robert C. Kolodny, director of research at the Reproductive Biology Research Foundation in St. Louis, has stated, "People have found it [swinging sex life] to be more enslaving than freeing. They came to realize, that on the contrary, it contributed little to their maturation and development as individuals." Kolodny said that these conclusions were based on several hundred clinical interviews with couples.

One other modification of sexual life-style encompasses those who have chosen to live together communally—allowing but not demanding shared sexuality. While a good deal of publicity was originally given to this particular life-style, it has not turned out to be a panacea for marriage problems. Frequently groups that started out with the objective of each member being sexually active with as many others in the group as she or he wished, discovered that the participants eventually tended to lapse into more or less lasting twosomes. It proved difficult to sustain relationships on the basis of randomness. Conflict in the commune, rather than utopia, was frequently the result.

Those who have counseled with married couples where infidelity has been involved have rarely heard either the husbands or wives express a wish to go through the experience all over again. It is a painfully traumatic situation, where persons may be giving various messages to their spouses: "I need help." "I feel uncherished." "Our relationship is not love nourished." "Something in me makes it impossible to reach out and respond to you." "I need reassurance of my value as a person."

Perhaps at first this unspoken plea for help—sometimes manifested in its rudimentary form by bickering, conflict, or withdrawl—went unheeded. Eventually the call for help became symbolically strident and was exercised in a form which could no longer be ignored—namely, adultery. Usually at this point such a feeling of betrayal and rejection arises that the doors for further communication are too often irrevocably closed. I have seen no jubilant partners at this point. There is only anguish. A grief process ensues which is very painful, for an emotional scalpel now severs one-fleshness into separate parts again. How could there not be trauma?

Sometimes these separated individuals are later heard to say in counseling: "I wish we hadn't given up." "I wish we had kept on trying." "I wish we had sought help at that point." What we are discovering, then, is that the sexual indiscretion was symptomatic of another manner of unfaithfulness. I believe that as a church we have been so concerned with the unchanging stance on marital fidelity of the flesh that we have winked at the erosion of the sanctified interpersonal relationship between a husband and wife. We have not realized, as we should, how the erosion can cause the infidelity. It is difficult to eliminate coldness, misunderstanding, harshness, criticalness, divisions of interests, lack of vitality (including sexual), and withdrawal from the marriage. These may make keeping the seventh commandment, in a narrow sense, seem "as easy as eating apple pie."

We have mentioned what may lead to marital infidelity and the type of injuries that it can cause. Perhaps we should give some thought to what one does when experiencing a desire to become sexually involved outside a marriage or when facing the fact that a spouse is unfaithful.

Probably few married persons at one time or another have not at least briefly been tempted to fantasize about an encounter of marital infidelity. Natural body response to ever-present stimuli should not astonish us. Emotions don't have principles—the person in whom they reside must provide these. When a person finds himself or herself responding repeatedly with favorable attitudes toward indulging these temptations to imaginative encounters, the time has come for some self-confronting thought.

I have often thought that if persons who get into affairs were to expend as much energy in working on their own marriages as they do in fantasizing, planning, and furtive activity, they could revitalize their "tired-blood" marital situations. "Cheating in marriage, simply put, infers taking what is wanted without regard to the common best interest of the marriage," says Dr. Natalia Shainess. She further states: "It is a common goal, common interests, and the nurturing of love by caring and concern for the partner, using self-discipline when occasionally necessary, which permit a marriage to grow. Without these, it is not much of a marriage—it is a living arrangement possibly convenient but not exciting, not 'soul food.' Nothing worthwhile is ever acquired easily."

A person in this situation should ask herself or himself the following questions:

"Why do I feel this way, when years ago I was convinced that I could happily pledge a lifetime of fidelity?"

"How have *I* changed—physically and emotionally?"

"Am I nuturing a love relationship in a way that leaves no doubt in my spouse's mind that she or he is an attractive, worthwhile person?"

"What makes me think this new relationship could be more lasting?"

"Have I discussed my feelings of dissatisfaction (however vague) with my spouse in calm, loving, nondefensive ways (this excludes blaming, pleading, sarcasm)?"

"Have I been willing to seek professional help for our problems? Or is the new car more attractive than counseling fees?"

And then, if one is a committed Christian, it would be important to ascertain how comfortable one would feel in asking God to bless this newly desirable liaison. This would infer explaining to God that it would be unlikely that He would have the ability to help bring healing happiness to the marriage one now intends to abandon.

Now let's talk about that second situation. What should one do when one learns that a spouse has been unfaithful. Perhaps we could highlight this by suggesting what a spouse should *not* do:

Do not get into a big dramatic scene which pulls out all of the stops (e.g., yelling, histrionics, threats of suicide), with the hope of frightening the other into some kind of compliance.

Do not insist that things be "hashed out" right here and now, regardless of the time of day or circumstances, when perhaps a cooling-off period of waiting would serve everyone's interests best.

Do not make threats of divorce, a vindictive financial settlement, alienation of children, parents, friends, or business associates as a punishment for this indiscretion.

Do not turn this exercise into a self-pitying session: "After all of these years, the best of my life, what did I ever do to deserve this?"

Do not beg and plead for another chance.

Do not call off the whole marriage right now with the statements which are so irretrievable: "I'll never forgive you for this," or "I could never trust you again."

Nothing should be done impulsively. Oh, it's true, you have no doubt heard others say or may have said yourself, "If anyone ever did that to me, that would be the end. Period!" But that seems to be a rather immature way of handling something as deeply involved as two peoples' lives have been. Much more is gained for all concerned by an opportunity to think through what might be involved. It would make a difference if this was a one-time fling or a momentary indiscretion, as compared to a long-term affair. An affair would seem to represent a protracted marital discontent, a different situation from a brief fling.

This "injured" spouse needs to take a good look at her or his partner. Have there been recent indications of depression, stress, or discontentment? Has the work situation provided few gratifications—where the spouse constantly feels unproductive or unappreciated? Have long-term goals failed to materialize—financial, professional, educational or family? Have a number of couples in their own peer group undergone divorce or other distress? These and other changes may have slowly and imperceptibly taken place without her or his coping responsibly with them.

But that is only part of this cognitive exercise. Now a self-examination becomes extremely important—and painful. However, it is a sign of Christian maturity when a person can confrontively ask questions of one's self and listen for honest answers. These should include these: How have *I* changed from the bride or groom in whom my spouse found delight? Am I as accepting, loving, and reassuring a person as I once was? Or have I grown to become unresponsive, uncommunicative, passive, and uninteresting? Do I endeavor to remain physically attractive, aesthetically and hygienically pleasing? What kind of "vibrations" do I give off when my spouse gives evidence of sexual interest? Do I send messages which indicate boredom, disinterest, sufferance, or disenchantment with the whole sexual experience? A complete and genuine investigative process will probably indicate that on both parts disloyalties could be recognized.

Dr. Spurgeon English has written, "I agree that if you can make the marriage beautiful, if you can be on the same wavelength and have the trust, interest, the love and respect that is desirable, an affair would be unnecessary." I believe that we have just been given a very acceptable formula for a Christian marriage. When either party in a violated marriage realizes that she or he may have become careless about her or his part in fulfilling that formula, how much better to rush to dialogue—alone or with appropriate helping persons—than to rush to separate.

Dr. English believes that adultery, when reacted to thoughtfully, can have an effect which is not negative. He feels that it can "cause both parties to be more aware of each other's needs, more sensitive to each other's feelings, more concerned about the other's happiness and emotional welfare. Having suffered and not wishing to repeat the suffering, they take better care of each other's emotional needs in the future." He further posits that if "there was little love in the marriage initially then a break-up is more prone to occur after adultery. If the spouses love each other and consider each other's feelings, they will generally sustain the emotional crisis of adultery, be more sensitive to each other, and their future relationship will be more improved. This takes considerable compassion, patience, forgiveness, and a reappraisal of the meaning and importance of a sexual relationship both within and outside of marriage." One might add that if all these qualities had been in the marriage as a constant, the pain of infidelity could have been avoided.

How often we are told by one spouse something reminiscent of the old plaint, "I can forgive, but I can't forget." But forgiveness by God's definition means remembering the offense no more. This human attitude must be difficult for the angels to understand, when they recall how much each of us must daily be forgiven for expressing a lack of Christian love in so many areas and particularly when they recall what Christ has redemptively forgiven us through His death. Forgiveness is not something that we generate from within ourselves any more than love is. Each is a gift from God's hand. True, adulterous behavior says the wrong things about God, but so does unwillingness to forgive. Christians have a great advantage in that God can and will grant them the grace of forgetting. And there is sufficient grace—God assures us of that. The act can be remembered only as one gives consent for it to remain in the mind.

One other issue should be touched on here, and that is this

question: "Should I tell my spouse that I have been unfaithful?" What ought a Christian to do? No handy formula exists which solves this problem. It sometimes becomes a question of which is the better of two evils—wounding an unsuspecting spouse (though many would question how a sensitive spouse could remain completely innocent of any emotional or physical indicators) or bearing the weight of unconfessed guilt.

If there ever was a time when the spouse would want to tear aside any possibility of self-deception, however painful, it is now. "What are my reasons for revealing my indiscretion?" The answer to this question must be carefully contemplated, probed, and ferreted. There are possible hidden agendas (conscious or unconscious) for confession that the questioner must try to discover. They include the following reasons:

Perhaps there is a feeling of wanting to "get even" with a spouse for a perception that emotional and sexual needs were never considered or understood.

There may be a need to share the hurt and anguish being felt, with the hope of thus diluting it.

There may be a desperate chance that she or he will be forgiven by the spouse when the person can't forgive herself or himself.

The spouse may really want out of the marriage but wishes to put the responsibility on the other—having a pretty clear idea that if the spouse realizes the adultery, the response would be to "get out." Then the "confessing" spouse can lament, "What else could I do? I tried."

The motive may be a means of showing a spouse how desirable she or he really is to someone else even if the spouse doesn't seem to appreciate the sexual appeal appropriately.

It would be best, it seems to me, to discuss this problem with a professional Christian counselor who might be able to see areas in which the person involved is blinded. If irreparable damage would result, it is possible that the offending party may have to bear the extra burden of knowledge alone.

Should confession be decided upon, no good end is served by a detailed report of what has gone on. Sometimes an "innocent" spouse demands one, feeling that it would help to know what he or she now only imagines. This situation again calls for outside counseling before yielding to wishes. Usually, the fewer details to dwell upon, the less problem in putting them from the mind.

We have dealt for one whole chapter on the stresses, pain, and problems caused by unfaithfulness in marriage. In five short words God tried to preserve us from all of this. His command—the seventh in His loving series—was not arbitrary and imperious. Rather, He loved us so much that He sought to build a protective hedge around our married love. Praise God for His omniscient wisdom!

Growing Older Sexually

In a recent professional journal a professor in human sexual behavior states that one in four of a group of university students he surveyed cannot imagine her or his parents being sexually active, and only one in thirteen could imagine grandparents engaging in sexual activity. (See *Medical Aspects of Human Sexuality*, October 1979, p. 11.) This would certainly indicate that, in the minds of most younger persons at least, sexual experience is no longer an option for "old folks." This latter group apparently includes people in their fifties and beyond. When Robert Browning stated (in "Rabbi Ben Ezra"), "Grow old along with me! / The best is yet to be," many people would be unwilling to concede that this includes sexuality.

Because this attitude is so prevalent—as indicated by remarks, ancedotes, and jokes (which I consider to be in poor taste)—older folks tend to be embarrassed about their needs and desires. Frequently they stifle these to fit the stereotype of a properly neutered senior citizen. How tragic! Sexual needs and pleasures are not metered by a calendar. There are, indeed, aspects that suggest that the sexual relationship between a husband and wife in later years may be more significant and more rewarding than at any time in their lives. No longer is the older couple concerned about the possibility of pregnancy. With the children having left home to start their own family cycles, distractions and preoccupations do not frustrate lovemaking desires. Over the years they have hopefully developed better communication, with a fuller expression of needs and desires. Some of the earlier inhibitions are now released, and both wife and husband can feel comfortable with freer expression of their sexuality.

Further, the years may have given them a sense of security and trust in one another which could not be as deeply present when they first married. Their lovemaking, as well as all the other areas of their intimacy, would be enhanced by an acceptance of one another as caring, demonstrative partners in this celebration of love. Through the years they will have learned to respond to one another's rhythms and reciprocations. While the expression of their love may not leap in white flames, yet it warms, comforts, and delights!

Unfortunately, many times late middle age becomes the prelude to declining sexual activity rather than remaining one of the most enduring parts of the relationship. Aside from the messages they have received from their environment, which infer that sexuality is inappropriate for the aging, physical changes begin to be felt. Unless these are not correctly anticipated and understood, they can add to the confusion felt at this time. I would like to talk about these changes for both women and men.

Female Changes in Later Years

It should be heartening for older women to realize that sexual desire persists in the majority of their peers. Longitudinal studies done at Duke University showed that for 75 percent of women in their seventies, sexual desire persisted.

As in most areas of bodily functioning, there will usually be some difference in response. But difference does not necessarily mean less joy. It is important for a woman to realize that these modifications do not mean that she is "past her prime" and going into sexual decline. Nor do they mean that her husband is not as capable of providing her with the stimulation she requires. Sometimes a woman sees herself as less desirable and less attractive. She believes this is also her husband's perception and interprets it as a diminishing of his ardor. Not so. The physiological signs of arousal simply do not take place as readily. Lubrication may be slower to accumlate, and there may also be less. This may sometimes call for artificial lubrication in the form of a water-soluble lubricating jelly. It is possible that stimulation of the sexually receptive parts of her body will need to be more prolonged. But this can only add to the total experience of pleasure at a time when the couple has more time to spend exclusively with one another.

Other changes of which a woman is seldom aware of (even when younger) will include less uterine elevation, less increase in vaginal canal size, fewer skin color changes, and less elasticity of the tissues. There may be changes in the labia major which include less cushioning of the mons due to loss of fatty tissue. This may call for more care for the sensitivity of the clitoris. But communication with one's spouse about body feelings during lovemaking will assist in working out whatever changes in stimulation may be called for.

While the orgasmic phase may be somewhat shortened, the resulting relaxation and feeling of well-being is equally satisfying. Occasionally postmenopausal women will experience tenderness and even pain during intercourse due to the thinning of the vaginal wall. This is due to a diminishing estrogen component. A woman experiencing this discomfort should consult her doctor immediately about the use of an estrogen cream to relieve this condition. It is gratifying to know that women who engage in regular sexual activity show fewer of the above problems. There is also some indication that a woman who remains interested in sexual interaction and engages in sexual activity may actually stimulate some estrogen production. (See Butler, *Love and Sex After Sixty*, p. 18.) The advice of most informed medical authorities for people approaching the sixties and going beyond is this: "Try to maintain your intellectual and sexual activities as long as possible."—Ruth and Edward Brecher, *An Analysis of Human Sexual Response*, p. 259.

Male Changes in Later Years

While concern for what a woman perceives as a dulling of her sexual abilities can provoke anxiety for her, it does not interfere with her physical ability to be a sexual partner. This is not true of her husband's experience. When he becomes preoccupied with the physical quality of his sexual functioning, he can actually worry an otherwise able body into sexual incompetence. Many times quite normal reactions are seen as inadequate—by prior standards—and this sets up a program of failure. For this reason it is very important for a man to be aware of the differences in his sexual response patterns so that he can accept these changes with equanimity rather than panic.

Since the changes in sexual functioning are as gradual as they are predictable, many times they can be unnoted or disregarded for a time. However, on some occasion when, because of fatigue, illness, or preoccupation, the genitals do not respond according to some pre-set norm, anxiety occurs. A man may feel he is "over the hill" and become despondent over his "performance."

Generally the readiness of erection is affected, and a man will note that it takes longer for his penis to become erect. What formerly happened in a few seconds, with appropriate stimuli, may be delayed to several minutes. It will also be noted that the penis is not as firm, straight, or large as it had been in his earlier days. None of these changes need interfere with a good sexual experience unless the concern over them causes psychological dysfunction. A delayed erection does not indicate that the erection will not be "sturdy and reliable, particularly if this was the pattern in earlier life."—Butler, *Love and Sex After Sixty,* p. 20.

Men who have formerly been troubled over ejaculating prematurely may indeed find this problem somewhat ameliorated, since the urgency to ejaculate with stimulation does diminish.

Some men who have noted a small amount of lubrication emitting from the penis prior to ejaculation (and this is not true of all men) will note that this fluid becomes diminished or disappears. Again this has little if any effect on sexual functioning. There will be a decrease in the amount of semen and in the vigor of its being expelled. But since conception is not desired generally, this does not affect sexual communication in an older couple.

An older man may notice that there is a briefer period of awareness—that moment of "inevitability"—just before ejaculation. The intensity of orgasm may undergo some changes, but this need not take away from the overall experience of love-play, intercourse, and afterglow. Probably one of the most significant changes is the length of the refractory period, which is the time lapse between one ejaculation and the ability to enter again into an intercourse experience. Where as a young man can, within a few minutes or hours, regain the penile ability to become erect, an older man will need to wait a longer period of time. His erection will become flaccid quite quickly after ejaculation. Neither of these changes in any way indicates impairment of the penis and its erectile capacity. Furthermore lovemaking is not limited to ejaculatory ability. Many older men have finally come to realize what women have known—a highly satisfactory sexual interlude can be experienced without orgasm. Loving, touching, closeness, and one-fleshness need not insist on the one-and-only ending of orgasm to make the interlude sexually fulfilling.

How wonderful, then, that a time when the changes in life-style through retirement, loss of a productive working role, loss of family and old friends, a husband and wife can still find pleasure in one another's touch, can still find status in one another's eyes, and still feel their masculinity and femininity enhanced through one another's sexual response. How typical of God's goodness to prolong this gift of sexuality throughout their years together.

Aging and Illness

Certain medical conditions frequently associated with aging can affect sexual functioning. Some of these are heart disease, hypertension, diabetes, disabling cancer, arthritis, anemia, Parkinsons's disease, prostate problems. Some types of surgery also cause a change in sexual patterns, either temporarily or permanently. Medications taken to control or treat these illnesses may have an effect on sexual capability as well.

It is not the purpose of this book to discuss these medical conditions. But should you note a change in sexual response or ability, you should consult a physician without delay. While the problem may be medically related, most physicians will realize that psychological overlay could complicate the situation, and they will be sensitive to the need for assistance in that area. No person should feel that the last word in this problem should be "Well, you have lived a good life and are probably ready to give up sex anyway" or "You are not as young as you used to be; what do you expect?"

When a lovemaking experience has been a proving ground rather than a shared intimacy, a lost erection and a missed orgasm, especially if repeated, can be seen as failure. And failure is frightening. Orgasm should not be thought of as the ultimate proof of sexual enjoyment. Nor should its absence be seen as an indication of the demise of intimacy. A couple will then just give up on that part of their communion. Even without problems of dysfunction, a norm of performance is too heavy a burden to carry. With physical problems it can become a disaster.

Couples need to take inventory of what they can still count on when illness or disability strikes. "Are there still good body feelings? Where? How can they be aroused? What positions are still comfortable, and how can we accomodate to one another in these? What times of day are most ideal from the standpoint of energy and the most freedom from discomfort? What caressing activities are the most pleasing?"

In conclusion, if both partners in this situation are encouraged every time they make love (which includes the whole gamut of sexual experience, not simply intercourse) to derive from the present experience a feeling of closeness and sensuousness without feeling driven to perform, if they can do this without a prejudgment as to what this episode must provide, and if they can go along with their God-given feelings, then every sexual experience will not devolve into a test situation. They can relax and let happen what will happen and derive pleasure from it. They can, indeed, still enjoy a one-flesh intimacy.

More Than Birds and Bees

Surely there has never been a parent who looked at a newborn baby and thought, "I am going to try to put roadblocks in the way of your ever enjoying a truly good sexual relationship when you marry. I am going to attempt to confuse you by my silences, my attitudes, and my words. I am going to avoid talking about sexuality at all, if that is possible. But if it becomes absolutely necessary to do so, I will make my remarks so vague, so hurried, that there will be no doubt in your mind that I am uncomfortable and reluctant, so that eventually you will leave me alone. That ought to take care of that!" I repeat, these thoughts surely could not be present in the mind of a parent, though in reality this is the scenario which too often follows.

It is unbecoming to be too hard on parents, for they usually reflect experiences with their own parents. But I am delighted to hear from some young parents that they are determined to give their children a different learning experience than they had in the sexual area. Things are looking up!

I believe that the first thing of importance to realize is that only a small part of our sex education is verbal and intended. Unless we have a good feeling about ourselves as sexual persons, words may even be coming out correctly, but our message may not be congruent. That is why this chapter is near the end of this book. Hopefully by now there may be a better understanding of this wonderful gift and a wholesome delight in what it can contribute to our personhood. That should make communication easier.

Certainly at birth, if not before, the script begins. Neonatologists, those who study newborns, have recently come to realize the importance of the freshly born babe's having a "bonding" experience with its parents. Many hospitals now provide a time immediately after birth for at least the mother and child to interact in a skin-to-skin situation for some minutes. The benefits are felt to be a healthier and more contented baby, with feelings of parental love being enhanced. Babies need to be held, cuddled and admired with hands, eyes, voices, and mouths. The good sensations this provides helps the little ones to establish a body awareness and also helps to give them a feeling of security and trust. All this begins to lay an early foundation for a good sexual experience in marriage, where these qualities of trust and feelings of security and body pleasure are of prime importance. When a baby is handled seldom, roughly, and without loving verbal stimulation, this begins to introduce a pattern for lack of sensitivity and a diminished appreciation for gentleness and warmth.

We spoke in chapter 4 of the influences during these early years. Perhaps it would not be out of the way to repeat here the necessity for not becoming anxious, agitated, or even punitive when an infant goes through the stages of touching it's body, which will almost certainly include the genital area. Evidences of displeasure or shame are not positive. A small child does not understand your moral concerns and therefore can only associate sexuality (or the part of their body which will later be involved in adult sexual activity) with unpleasantness when the only response recalled is frowns, stern or horrified faces, and comments such as "nasty," "dirty," "naughty." This must be particularly puzzling when senses report that pleasant sensations *are* felt in the genital area. What confusion!

When the infant enters childhood at about two years, new opportunities are presented for parents to educate for a healthy attitude toward sexuality. As the little ones begin to note differences in male and female bodies and begin to associate word names with various parts of their anatomy, they have a right to be given correct information. Questions should be answered simply and to the point. A question which wonders why baby brother has a penis does not demand a whole treatise on sexuality. A simple answer which states, "That is brother's penis. Little boys have penises, and little girls have vaginas. Someone has suggested that a statement like "Boys are fancy on the outside and girls on the inside" was comforting to their daughter who thought she had either lost part of her anatomy or had somehow been slighted. This feeling of inferiority on the part of a little girl can be fostered without an explanation as to her body counterpart to the penis.

Sometimes parents feel that the less they talk about these sexual aspects the better it will be for their children. It may, in fact, keep them "pure" longer. This may be an interesting admission on the part of the parents that they see sexuality as sordid rather than sacred.

I was interested to read in *The Health Reformer* for January 1873 an article endorsed by Ellen White. In fact, Mrs. White's note to the columns stated, "The following article from the *Herald of Health* should be carefully read and thoughtfully pondered." The author addressed her readers thus: "I write unto you, mothers, that you may purify the world." In the course of the article she decried the ignorance among girls about their "physical constitution and development." She continued:

"Why is this? Is it because the laws which govern our bodies, our whole lives are impure, unworthy to be studied? Do we thus regard our Heavenly Father? Should we thus degrade his words?

"These laws are the same as those which govern the lives of plants and animals. Children are taught of those—taught to look with admiration and delight at the development of the beautiful blossom from the tiny germ, and its final transformation into the perfect flower and fruit, but of themselves, 'God's noblest work,' they are left in ignorance. Better far, that as little children, they should be taught of their own structure and development, as of the plants and trees, and taught to trace it in God's loving mind and hand, than at the age when they most need care and sympathy, when mysterious feelings are pressing upon them, and the great questions of life arise before them, that they should be forced to learn from playmates those things which it should be a mother's privilege to teach, and of the sacredness of which they cannot have too high a conception!"

Perhaps some are thinking, "That's just how I feel; sex education should be in the home and not in the school." Unfortunately, it is so seldom in the home that unless the school makes some provision, a child may never be made aware of the facts connected with the biological aspects of sexuality. This is certainly not the ideal, for sexuality taught as a biological function only is certainly not the best sex education. But even that is better than nothing. When homes can provide loving, sensitive information, having some sex education in the school, unless very much out of balance, can be a means of further and continued communication between parents and children as they discuss together what the children are hearing in their classes.

Before a child enters school, certain basic concepts should already be in mind. Frequently parents make the error of thinking that at some magic moment a child is ready to have the whole sexual-educational block. Perhaps a mother becomes concerned that menstruation is the next developmental milepost, or a boy is heard to use a "bad" word—sometimes without knowledge of its meaning. *Now,* it is felt, is the time for that important "talk."

Not so. A continuous unfolding of knowledge in keeping with a child's natural curiosity and his ability to understand is far preferable. Occasionally a parent will state, almost in relief, "Well, my child hasn't asked any questions at all; so I guess she [or he] is not ready."

This may not be the case. The child may be picking up the parent's discomfort in talking about sexual things. This may have been absorbed so early in life that there is no conscious appreciation of it by either parent or child. Or perhaps the parents have not been listening carefully to small-child remarks or questions. Seemingly casual statements like "Johnny's dog is going to have puppies" or "I saw Mary's mommy put her on the potty" could infer that some questions are buzzing through a small mind. Not all important questions come in the classical form, "Where do babies come from?" Parents need to alert themselves to natural opportunities to talk about sexual concerns.

Before their children are enrolled in school, parents should have discussed these basic concepts with them: correct names for body parts, correct names for elimination, correct names for the parts which are different in girls' and boys' bodies, the fact that the human baby develops inside the mother in the mother's uterus (not "tummy"), and the nurturing role mothers have in breast-feeding.

In the next few years the child should learn about the development of the egg cell in the mother's body and the sperm cell in the father's. The "birds-and-bees" concept is much more complicated for a child than sperm-and-egg concept as demonstrated first in the bodies of animals, then of humans.

This process of internal fertilization is one which many

parents find difficult to explain. The theme of the love of mothers and fathers for one another and their desire to express their love in being very close to each other is usually understandable to children.

I say "usually" because in homes where mothers and fathers do not demonstrate love and tenderness to one another, this theme can be a missing ingredient, impossible to explain. How important it is for the whole educational plan to be based on love and consideration between parents. It is not simply a pretty phrase, "the best thing mothers and fathers can do for their children is to love one another." It is a truism which is particularly applicable to helping children to get a well-balanced and sensitive picture of sexuality, always associated in their minds with love, commitment, and responsibility.

When the child can realize that loving one another is shown in wanting to be close, it is usually comfortable to explain that in this love there is a desire to have someone else in the family with whom to share that love. In words suited to the child's own vocabulary, the parent should carefully explain that daddy puts into mommy's body a very important cell (or seed). He does this by placing his penis in the place God planned for it to fit, in her vagina. They do this when they are loving one another in a very special way that God designed only for mommies and daddies—just as there are very special ways of hugging and loving for boys and girls and their mommies and daddies. This will usually be sufficient for the time. Since the child already has the information that girls have vaginas so that someday they can be mothers and boys have penises so that someday they can be fathers, this information will usually be easy for the child to accept and understand.

Once the parents have been able to give this information without the world's caving in (and sometimes one gets the feeling that this is exactly what may happen if sexuality is discussed freely!), they begin to feel more comfortable and can become effective communicators in this sensitive area.

A good number of fine books written for children explain these important concepts with pictures and diagrams. Parents might consider spending several hours at a bookstore and library looking over these books together. Some are not as sensitively done as others, or their illustrations may be less tasteful. For this reason I suggest parents page through each prospective book carefully before bringing it home. Reading together is a fine way to build up rapport between parent and child, and it can assist in stimulating discussion. I am *not* in favor of parents' using the book as the sole educational instrument! That's a bit of a cop-out! It does not do nearly as much for the relationship of parents and child as does family discussion. How important it is to build *communication,* so that children can feel not only comfortable but willing, even eager, to ask questions, relate anecdotes and reveal confusions which they inevitably face in their growing-up years. How many adolescents might have been spared bewilderment, anxiety, and even anguish if they had felt secure in the presence of warm and accepting parents who are consistently ready to discuss—undefensively and unjudgmentally and in a spirit of exploration—any topic relating to their feelings and understanding of sexuality. Parents should strive for this goal under God's direction and blessing.

By puberty each child should have a clear picture of the miracle of reproduction and maternal care. Boys as well as girls should understand the onset of menstruation as a natural part of a girl's growing up. And girls as well as boys should understand nocturnal emission as a natural part of a boy's growing up. No loving parents should be willing to run the risk of these events happening without a thorough preparation, which includes not only the physiological aspects, but also the appreciation of this entrance into womanhood and manhood. What grateful comments I have heard from young people who have been prepared for these experiences! And how much easier it is to espouse the values of parents who have had a significant part in discussing these "great questions of life" with their children.

Under these circumstances adolescents, who usually go through a confusing and stormy time at this development stage, will have a greater sense of security in feeling their parents' love and interest. Many times ignorance of accurate sexual knowledge rather than a clear understanding of themselves causes young people in their curiosity to experiment in ways which lead to misguided behavior. Since so little consensus exists among even respected "authorities" as to the definition of proper sexual conduct, young people seek a safe place where they can discuss conflicting ideas.

Sometimes these discussions may be initiated in the form of talking about their friends: "Mary and Johnny pet a lot at her house while her parents are at work." "One of the kids at school thinks she's pregnant, and she's really worried."

One way to stop all further communication would be to reply in the first instance, "If they're not careful, they'll get into real trouble—don't you let me catch you doing that." Or in the second, "I don't know what kids expect when they go steady at fifteen; she'll probably ruin her whole life. If any child of mine did that, I'd blow sky-high."

But displays of protestations, dire threats, and warnings are ineffective. Compare the following responses to those same remarks: "It sounds like you have some feelings about that." "She really must be feeling quite worried; it must be pretty hard for her to know what to do. What do you think she should do?"

After open, nonintimidating sessions, the parents can effectively communicate the way they see things, what the Christian stand would be in different cases, their desire for their children with respect to their sexual choices, and the happiness they want these choices to bring to them. God's blessing will rest on this type of interaction. I believe that rich benefits will result, not only in more responsible behavior during these adolescent years, but in enhanced sexual adjustment in their children's marriages.

Other issues of sex education are usually more difficult to bring into communication. The scope of this book does not include such topics as exhibitionism, homosexuality, molestation, rape, and other harmful sexual practices. When children are faced with these types of experiences, the parents should seek appropriate counseling resources. If a parent can keep the initial reactions to such reports from being too emotionally laden, the child will generally achieve a more positive resolution of the trauma that could result. Both parents and the child should be involved in the therapy process.

Another topic should be included in our discussion of education, one which still manages to stir up a good deal of controversy among sincere Christian people. And that is the subject of masturbation. This sexual topic is not mentioned in the Bible, and what is said here is not meant to be an authoritative statement. But perhaps it can help sort out some of the confusing ideas surrounding this issue.

In beginning, I would like to point out what masturbation is *not*. It is not the curious examination of her or his own genitals by a small child. (Nothing is more natural than for infants or children to have an inquisitive interest in each part of their own bodies and therefore to use the skills of touching—the same skills which are not questioned when another part of the environment is being "studied.") Nor is it the nocturnal emission phenomenon, which is the involuntary release of seminal fluid experienced by males as a release from sexual tension. (Too often boys have been shamed and accused of dark deeds when their bodies have taken over this function. Sometimes young men have suffered needless remorse and guilt when they have experienced nocturnal emissions and have felt this to be evidence of their impurity.)

Again, masturbation is not something husbands and wives do to each other. On occasions the term "mutal masturbation" is taken to mean the stimulation and arousal of one another's body. This is not correct. Masturbation is an act of self-stimulation to the point of sexual climax. It is a solo and lone activity involving the body of one person. Perhaps this is why it offends the sensibilities of some people. Since sexual communication is a matter of beautiful body communication between two people and since it is a relationship-enhancing opportunity, sexuality misses the mark when it is cheated of this communion, this sharing and joining.

One last thing—masturbation is not onanism or "the spilling of seed." This act is mentioned in the Bible, and sometimes it is confused with masturbation. In this instance Onan was unwilling to impregnate his widowed sister-in-law for the purpose of raising up progeny for his deceased brother. (See the *Seventh-day Adventist Bible Dictionary*, p. 79.)

At times throughout history well-meaning parents have sometimes gone to great lengths to keep their children from stumbling upon or indulging in any body-touching pleasures. Aside from dire threats, which could only be effective for children old enough to fear the dreadful consequences attributed to masturbation, various physical restraints were used. On record such means included the tying of hands and legs to bedposts, aluminum mittens, and metal contrivances over the genitals, some of which employed points which would dig into the flesh of the penis if it became erect.

Within the ranks of the Seventh-day Adventists various attitudes exist toward masturbation. Some feel that though the Bible is silent on this matter, Ellen White has written with sufficient clarity to convince them that she is speaking of masturbation when she talks of "secret vice," "self-abuse" and other such phrases. These indeed were common terms of the time for masturbation. In Webster's International Dictionary of 1864-84, however, there were three meanings given for the term *self-abuse*. In the order given, I list them here: (1) the abuse of one's own self, power, or faculties; (2) self-deception, delusions; (3) masturbation, onanism, self-pollution.

I am not proposing here that Ellen White was NOT speaking of masturbation in these instances. I am only suggesting it is wise to be careful what we attribute to the words of any author in view of contemporary choices.

Let us spend just a few moments on some of the conditions which Ellen White did attribute to self-abuse. These seem to be categorized into four different areas:

1. Physical findings: Headaches, dizziness, wakefulness, feverishness, exhaustion, nervousness, pain, loss of appetite, and a number of specific diseases.

2. Intellectual signs: Forgetfulness, inattention, idiocy, and a brain derangement most of which she attributed to problems with the "fine nerves of the brain."

3. Emotional effects: Apathy, gloom, sadness, jealousy, rebellion against parental authority, and premature marriage.

4. Spiritual conditions: Death to spiritual matters, destruction of high resolve and earnest endeavor, and removal of oneself from holy influence.

One cannot but be impressed when reading *An Appeal to Mothers, Child Guidance* (section 16), and *Testimonies* (vol. 2, pp. 346-411, 468-471, 481) how many times she mentions the word "mind" as though more were involved in the mind that in the purely physical. She was more concerned with thought processes: attitudes, fantasies, etc. Let me record here a few of these: "The effects are not the same on all minds." "Corrupting the mind." "Impure thoughts seize and control the imagination and fascinate the mind." "The first work of reform is to purify the imagination." "The mind is to be stimulated in favor of the right." "The mind takes pleasure in contemplating the scenes which awake base passion." "Corrupt imagination."

Ellen White further seems to indicate that this practice of self-abuse has more dire effects at different times of life: "The young indulge to quite an extent in this vice before the age of puberty without experiencing to any great degree the evil results upon the constitution. But at this critical period, while merging into manhood and womanhood, nature makes them feel the violation of her laws."—*An Appeal to Mothers*, p. 7. (Published in 1864.)

Another group of sincere Seventh-day Adventist Christians, who are somewhat embarrassed at Ellen White's statements as they are applied to masturbation, are prepared to opine that since no prophet is infallible (a statement she in fact made about herself), here is certainly an area in which she has been incorrect (following the thinking of her time). And since she said virtually nothing about this in the last years of her ministry, perhaps her views had changed somewhat. There is a feeling among others that the conditions attributed to self-abuse are so amplified and overstated that she leaves a credibility gap. Were all the people who masturbated, occasionally to regularly, to suffer the physical effects mentioned, they estimate from current statistics there would not be enough people left to take care of them.

It seems important at this point to recall that many other statements Ellen White made in the area of health predictions seemed unrealisitic and exaggerated before science corroborated them—e.g., cancer being caused by a virus and the dangers of smoking, overeating, and the overuse of fats and sugars and salt. While many times she did not understand the medical dynamics by which these words would prove to be confirmed, we can see her counsel vindicated. It seems worthwhile to remind ourselves that medical knowledge at any point is indeed not perfected. I have come to this conclusion for myself. Either *Ellen White* didn't know what she was talking about when she made the statements on self-abuse, or *we* do not know what *she* was talking about. I have far too much confidence in the messages of this remarkable woman to believe the former. I am convinced of the latter. Masturbation is not the simplistic phenomenon we sometimes take it to be. There are many aspects to consider. Let's employ the continuum concept. I see this continuum as having a simple physical relief on one extreme and pathological obsession on the other. Somewhere between will be a completely hedonistic self-love experience, including emotional and environmental setups and extensive fantasy. We would have to include frantic, compulsive masturbation somewhere in there, along with a lonely, withdrawn, repetitive experience.

Is any of us insightful enough to know exactly what point on the continuum she was referring to in any one of her statements? Certainly many respectable medical authorities feel that continuous, repetitive, compulsive masturbation may have pathological components. Was this her reference point? Was she referring to a fantasy experience which is unfaithful to a spouse? I don't know. I can't accept that anyone else can positively state so either.

Parents are frequently concerned, and rightly so, when children seem to be spending inordinate time and energy in genital play and masturbation. They will need to determine what this experience may be indicating. Is the child insecure, worried, bored? Is there some tension in the home atmosphere which gives a sense of rejection with resultant anxiety and restlessness? Does hostility, subtle undermining, or fighting between the parents give a sense of anxiety and restlessness? Punishing and shaming may only intensify the need to find a good body feeling. Parents would do better to evaluate the home atmosphere, the childhood pressures felt, and to seek to promote a more accepting, loving relationship between parents, as well as between each parent and the child.

In summary of this topic, I would like to repeat my belief that God's ideal for the ultimate of sexual expression is an experience of mutuality and one-fleshness between a wife and husband. I would hope that others might work out their philosophies in the manner I have found to be best—much study, reasoning, and prayer. On issues where we do not have a definitive biblical word and where there is a possibility of misunderstandings in our other authoritative source, I wonder if it is not unbecoming to become dogmatic on a point. By dogmatic I mean taking a position in an arrogant manner which brooks no discussion. As sisters and brothers in a pilgrimage which seeks to bring us closer and closer to God's ideal for our lives, let there be room for thoughtful, loving discussion on these important issues.

As Christian parents interact with their children from the earliest moments on, sharing with them the pleasures of loving demonstrations of caring, touching, and enfolding, instructing their children about sexuality in all of its aspects can become an enriching experience for all. So when a small child begins to "ask questions," rather than feeling uneasy, let us welcome these as opportunities to begin a dialogue which should lead to enhancement of the parent-child relationship and later to enhancement of the child's own marital relationship.

Thoughts on Happier Honeymoons

The first month of a marriage is called the "honeymoon" from an old idea that the first month (moon) is the sweetest. "Honeymoon" implies that the idealized, romantic expectation of the hours and days immediately following the wedding ceremony have a special quality of sweetness and sentimentality. What expectations are wrapped up in this magic time—the time between the vows and the verity!

The first month following the wedding was once considered a time of holiday or vacation spent together by a newly married couple. Indeed an entire month certainly seems preferable to the rush of several days away—jammed between the traditional busyness preceding a wedding and the return to a schedule crowded with settling into a new home and getting back to work or school.

The Bible stretches this time even further. "If a man has recently married, he must not be sent to war or have any other duty [this is sometimes amplified to include business or public service] laid on him. For one year he is to be free to stay home and bring happiness to the wife he has married." Deuteronomy 24:5, NIV. Now that sounds like a splendid antidote to marriages which get off to a poor start!

While some couples do look back on their honeymoons with nothing but pleasure, many others feel that this time might have more significantly promoted initial marital happiness. Whatever the situation before marriage, it now undergoes significant status changes during this culturally approved time spent alone. Couples whose basic knowledge of one another has been fragmentary now meet values, attitudes, and behavior quirks without the protection of "time off." Even those who have known one another through the traditional courtship and engagement "rites of passage" are sometimes surprised when the party atmosphere is over. The nitty-gritty of day-to-day living can do wonders to a fantasy. Even some couples who have lived together before marriage can be surprised at the difference in their feelings derived through their new total commitment as compared to their previous, cautious, tentative relationship.

So far, I have been speaking generally. This is by design. I have grown wary of jokes and anecdotes which depict the honeymoon as a nearly continuous round of sexuality. There is much more to this period of bonding between two people. The honeymoon can be a significant and worthwhile exploration of the many other facets of this union. However much this aspect of the honeymoon may be overplayed in popular literature and expression, to ignore that there is a great interest in and longing for the completion of the union of a bride and groom is not only unrealistic but undesirable. So since this book is directed to enhancing the sexual experience of a marital pair, something on beginnings seems called for.

Each member of this newly composed doublet brings a set of concerns to this occasion. For the bride it might include (1) fear of not reacting properly to her groom's lovemaking; (2) fear of displaying her body, which she may not feel good about; (3) fear of discomfort or even pain; (4) fear of not pleasing her lover by her actions.

For his part the groom may be going through his own special worries. These may include (1) what his bride will think of his body; (2) whether his sexual skills will be adequate; (3) whether he will be able to meet his bride's expectations of lovemaking; (4) whether he will be able to meet his own expectations; (5) whether he will be able to meet the stereotyped expectations of his peers; (6) what will happen if he ejaculates prematurely—and what she will think; or (7) what will happen if his anxiety precludes a good erection.

The amount of emotional energy expended in this type of anxiety would no doubt be impossible to measure! In an effort to diminish at least some of this honeymoon anxiety, I have stated here a number of suggestions. I will list these as though I were talking to the young couple planning marriage.

1. Plan in advance to have several premarital counseling sessions, either with a group or individually—or preferably both. This experience will help you to understand one another better, to talk over your expectations of all aspects of marriage, and to feel emotionally close to one another without hidden agendas. These sessions are sometimes offered by churches, schools, or private counselors.

2. Be certain that at least one of these sessions will be devoted to exploring your sexual norms, ideals, and values. Surprises in this area on a honeymoon can be devastating.

3. Use one of these sessions in discussing the congruence of your spiritual values. Simply belonging to the same church does not guarantee agreement on issues of life-style, the importance to each of a religious commitment, and the perceptions of each regarding the spirituality of sexuality.

4. Learn the anatomy and physiology of sexuality. An organism so exquisitely crafted as the human deserves your study and appreciation.

5. Obtain a physical examination for each. Don't try to talk your physician out of this intimidating experience. In all

probability, there will be no physical problems, but you won't know this for certain until you have been examined. Very few brides, for instance, need to be concerned about an imperforate hymen (one without opening) or even a reluctant one. But this condition does exist in a few women, even in this day of tampon use. When an imperforated hymen is discovered on a honeymoon through trial and error, very detrimental effects on future physical intimacy can result.

6. Plan for contraception well in advance. You will want to feel secure, comfortable, and at ease about the method you choose together. Some methods will demand prior attention to be effective at honeymoon time. I believe it is important for the prospective bride and groom to plan their contraception method and understand one another's feelings. Contraception is not simply a *female* responsibility; it is a *couple's* responsibility.

7. Groom, don't rush your bride out of her negligee! She may have spent hours finding just the right style, color, and trim! This purchase was much different from purchasing a plebian pair of pajamas! She is no doubt anxious to know if her choice pleases you. Remark about it!

8. Also groom, don't feel pressured to prove your sexual prowess the first or even the second night. That may sound like unrealistic advice! But some women have told me that one of the dearest memories of their groom was his suggestion that they simply relax and sleep in one another's arms the first night or so of their honeymoon. The frenzied activity of showers, wedding plans, last-minute exertions all took so much physical and emotional energy that it was difficult suddenly to become relaxed and expectant. This suggestion did not make the groom seem one whit less "manly" to his bride; in fact, it enhanced his masculinity in her eyes. Before you begin to feel sympathy for the patient groom, let me tell you that grooms have suggested that their own comfort level would have been raised

if they had felt it acceptable to make such a suggestion.

This brings me to suggest that this very idea might be discussed in advance. "What are our expectations for our wedding night?" When all the circumstances are taken into consideration, a couple can make a joint decision which may or may not include intercourse. The most important thing to come from the dialogue may not even be a rigid idea of what is expected, but may indeed be the feeling of concern and caring each feels is coming from the other.

9. Take along a tube of water-soluble lubricating jelly. While lubrication is probably going to be comfortably forthcoming when arousal occurs, the anxiety and apprehension which might be present could cause a delay or diminution of this secretion initially. Vaseline jelly is not a good substitute; nor is lotion or face cream.

10. You may want to take along a candle for atmosphere. A scented one may be even more appreciated. It is generally more romantic than a slit of light from a door left ajar. A book of love poetry will be a nice addition to an evening of love expression sometime during the honeymoon. Of course, a must is the love poetry of Solomon and his bride in the Song of Solomon. This type of activity begins to make communication about sexuality seem more natural.

11. Be aware of the condition so common as to be known as "honeymoon cystitis." This would consist of a burning, urgent feeling of urination for the bride. The bladder opening is so close to the vaginal opening that sometimes there can be irritation and a slight infection. Treatment for this would consist of drinking quarts of water, hot tub baths to soothe the named area, and, for a day or two during the discomfort, concentration on lovemaking activities which do not include intromission. If this condition does not respond within twenty-four hours to the above regime, consult a doctor, since there is medication which can bring relief.

12. Try to concentrate on experiencing, not on performing. This is good advice for a lifetime of sexuality, and the couple who begins to learn that art of loving early on has many good things to look forward to in this part of their sharing. In this area there are no norms to look forward to, no norms to live up to. No one else's honeymoon experiences need be your goal. You are two individual responders. Your love experience is yours and yours alone. Nor do you have to report on it to anyone or answer any personal questions about it. Many women, and men too, have felt betrayed and sometimes angry when they have heard from others that their spouse had disclosed some details of their sexual experience during their honeymoon, either in jest or seriously. Questions from inquisitive and sometimes insensitive people can be turned aside effectively but pleasantly.

Generally, it is more relaxing to have one set destination for the honeymoon period, rather than a full and hurried schedule. Packing and repacking, hurrying to meet varied deadlines (and new relatives!) sometimes takes away from the relaxation which can enhance sexual communication and all other aspects of intimacy.

To conclude, if couples can keep in mind that a honeymoon is only the beginning of life together, perhaps their expectations can be tailored to match this mere inauguration time. Lovemaking, relating to one another in a caring, sensitive way—these are the arts which are only beginning to be explored in these first weeks. Keeping a perspective on this can help these lovers to look forward to a lifetime of blending their lives together with increasing skills and enhanced sensitivities. God planned marriage to be a lifelong adventure in loving, which only begins to unfold on the honeymoon.

Temple Gairdner, great mission worker throughout his life, wrote these words in his diary as he prepared for his wedding day. They are worth repeating here:

That I may come near to her
  draw me nearer to Thee than to her;
that I may know her,
  make me to know Thee more than her;
that I may love her with the
  perfect love of a perfectly whole heart,
  cause me to love Thee more than her
  and most of all.

That nothing may be between me and her,
  be Thou between us every moment.
That we may be constantly together,
  draw us into separate loneliness with Thyself.
And when we meet breast to breast, O God,
  let it be upon Thine own.

"Prologue II"

Yes, I realize that a prologue is intended to be an introduction, a preliminary. My *New World Dictionary* calls "prologue" a foreshadowing of greater events. I like that. For though this is the book's last chapter, my hope is that it will indeed be a prologue for the enrichment of the sexual experience of wives and husbands, present and future.

If I were asked to sum up the most imperative components of a fulfilling sexual relationship in three words, I would say communication, intimacy, and relationship. One actually leads to the other. One of the goals of this book is to open up communication on sexual concerns between wives and husbands. I suggest that this might be accomplished by reading and discussing together what each has felt the messages of this book to be. Trying to second-guess what the other might be thinking and feeling is not only nonproductive, but it is also downright dangerous. No wedding vows include a pledge to be able to read the other's mind. To believe that I can or to think that my spouse should is to deny the complexity of our thought processes. It would be a simplistic, uninteresting, and chaotic world if we had the capability of knowing one another's thoughts and motives at all times. God did not create us thus.

Flourishing communication includes a willingness to listen

as well as to speak. It also presupposes an openness to ideas and an undefensive attitude (at least relatively so!) when presented with different concepts and sentiments. A wife and husband in a loving relationship which is consistently nourished by experiences and demonstrations of caring and concern will be able to enter into this kind of dialogue and to thrive on it. What joy to be able to discuss together the growing delights awaiting them in this God-ordained union!

Being increasingly able to participate in this type of openness can lead the way to a higher sense of intimacy. We spoke in chapter 6 of intimacy on several levels. A couple who have only physical approximation of bodies without the other components of togetherness cannot even be considered to be intimate. Intimacy denotes a closeness of whole persons. This type of experience reflects the root meaning of the word *within*. When two lovers are "within" one another's life boundaries, they are sharing, at a level unique to the marital relationship, a space not open to others. The emotions will be bound together in a rapport which is consistently nourished by loving interest in one another's ideas, values, choices, and goals.

Sexual intimacy, then, is not a thing of itself, reserved for intercourse only. It begins in the morning with pleasant, considerate communication. It thrives on a parting ritual which includes an embrace and a loving verbal send-off. In passing, I will share with you here what the result of such a morning rite might be expected to contribute. A delightful report was released by a West German research team. The team discovered that "men who kiss their wives before leaving for work in the morning enjoy better health, live longer and earn more money. . . . The morning kiss isn't just another kiss. It's the kiss that starts the day for both husband and wife. It is probably the most important kiss of the day." The study revealed that 87 percent of top business executives interviewed kissed their wives every morning. "A husband who kisses his wife begins the day with a positive attitude," Dr. Albert Szabo stated. (See *World*, July 31, 1977.) No doubt his wife shares that positive attitude, and the whole day can be experienced in a frame of mind which looks forward to being together again.

Throughout the day also thoughts can be drawn together. An occasional phone call when the work situation is appropriate, a note in a lunch box (or left on the counter for the spouse at home) which shares a personal sentiment creates between lovers bonds which enhance their feelings of closeness. As they think of one another during the day, these lovers may be placing in memory an anecdote to share, an experience to recall. Reporting a triumph or joy is not more important than sharing a disappointment or a put-down that was part of the day's quota of events. Where else should one be able to expose inner feelings and expect an empathetic response? And where else should the response be as spontaneous, as accepting, as healing?

The homecoming can also convey a message of caring. Does an engaged couple generally greet one another casually, fretfully, or disinterestedly? Perhaps the reason that some marriages tend to "cool off" may have to do with the amount of energy invested in them. Putting aside for the moment whatever the at-home spouse is engaged in (and with dual career families, it could be either the wife or husband who arrives home first) to greet one another with enthusiasm and warmth is a good time investment. A few moments of time out to embrace, kiss, establish eye contact, and to speak a few words of greeting can make for a good beginning of an evening together.

These two components, then—open, accepting communication and cherished intimacies on a variety of levels—are the basic ingredients for that marital togetherness which leads to an enhanced love relationship. Couples can transform an ordinary, obligatory-type sexual experience into joyous onefleshness when fore-experiences are enriched.

We started this book with God blessing Eve and Adam in the Garden. I would like to conclude it by suggesting that God's centrality in the relationships between husbands and wives makes it possible for Him to bless marriages in this marred world. Through God's abiding love we are imparted the power to love one another. We are given an understanding of the all-embracing quality of love. Perhaps we can say that the closer we come to realizing the completeness, the lastingness, the unconditionalness and steadfast devotion of God's love for us—entering into it and experiencing it as a daily communion for which we long and from which we do not wish to be drawn away—then the nearer we come to God's ideal for the love we experience with our earthly lover. "When human sexuality is expressed ordinately, responsibly, personally, faithfully, and with the urgent desire to share rather than to possess, it is indeed an appropriate symbol for the 'mystical union which is betwixt Christ and his Church' and for the relationship of finite persons to their Creator."—W. Norman Pittenger, "Toward a Christian Theology of Sexuality," *Union Seminary Quarterly Review,* vol. 30, Winter-Summer 1975, p. 129.

The sexual oneness God intended for our femaleness and maleness can indeed be a sanctified, and at the same time, a joyous delight. Think of this. Talk of it. Thank God for it. And rejoice with the bride and groom as they sing their song of songs:

> Let us go early to the vineyards
>   to see if the vines have budded
> if their blossoms have opened
>   and if the pomegranates are in bloom—
>   there will I give you my love.
>
> Song of Solomon